INSIGHT COMPACT GUIDE

MALLORCA

Compact Guide: Mallorca is the ideal quick-reference guide to this popular and startlingly beautiful island. It tells you all you need to know about the island's attractions, contrasting the sophistication of its capital, Palma, with the simplicity of its mountain villages, the bustle of its best resorts with the serenity of its monasteries and hermitages.

This is one of more than 100 titles in Insight Guides' series of pocket-sized, easy-to-use guidebooks edited for the independent-minded traveller. Compact Guides are in essence travel encyclopedias in miniature, designed to be comprehensive yet portable, as well as up-to-date and authoritative.

GW00371693

Star Attractions

An instant reference to some of Mallorca's most popular tourist attractions to help you on your way.

Palma Cathedral p17

Arab baths p21

Miró sculpture p25

Valldemossa p34

El Colomer panorama p51

Port d'Alcúdia p52

Inca market p58

Capocorb Vell p67

Cala Millor p76

Cap Gros lighthouse p46

Muro p78

Mallorca

Mallorca – a World within an Island

Opposite: the coast at Banyalbufar

The beach at Port de Sóller

Steep rocky coasts, seemingly endless sandy beaches, large tracts of marshland, high mountain ranges sloping down to fertile plains, an amazingly varied landscape, Mallorca is a self-contained world in its own right. Despite its relatively small surface area, the island's contrasts are stunning: the wild Serra de Tramuntana with its winding roads and sleepy mountain villages; the fragrant orange groves of the Sóller Valley; the terraced gardens around Banyalbufar with their gnarled, 1,000-year-old olive trees; the picturesque fishing villages of Porto Colom and Cala Figuera; the ancient stone walls separating the fields of apricots; almonds and potatoes in the island's interior. Mallorca's broad plains and gentle valleys are full of vineyards, and there are olive and fig trees everywhere.

Figs ripen in the sun

A good way of tackling the island is simply to strike off into the wild blue yonder, either by car or bicycle, far away from the signposted routes. There is always another quiet little part of the island waiting to be discovered – particularly in spring or autumn. Visit the picturesque villages of the interior, and travel up through forests of pine and oak to silent hermitages and down to peaceful coves. Admire impressive country estates and elegant Moorish gardens, and experience the noisy fiestas in honour of the local patron saints as well as the bustle of the colourful weekly markets. Take a stroll along the narrow streets of the capital, Palma, and around a few of its art galleries before sampling some delicious Mallorcan cuisine in a cool *celler* or relaxing in an old-fashioned coffee-house.

Relaxing in a Palma café

Volumes have been written on the evils of mass tourism, but anyone who simply leaves the crowded strips of coastline behind and heads inland will soon discover the original, unspoilt Mallorca, with its hidden bays, magnificent stretches of natural landscape and rich, cultural heritage.

Position and size

The Balearic Islands, an archipelago of five islands – Mallorca, Menorca, Ibiza, Formentera and the tiny Cabrera – lie off the northeastern coast of Spain. The archipelago covers a total surface area of 5,014sq km (1,935sq miles), and Mallorca is the largest (3,640sq km/1,405sq miles). The narrowest section of Mallorca, between the broad bays of Alcúdia and Pollença in the north and Palma Bay in the south, measures just 50km (31 miles); the distance between Cap de Sa Mola in the southwest and Capdepera in the northeast is around 100km (62 miles). The island's varied coastline, with its high cliffs, tiny pebble beaches and broad sandy bays, has a total length of 554km (344 miles).

Geological development

Bizarre rock formations, deep ravines, sedimentary rocks, sandy beaches, cliffs and caves all point to Mallorca's eventful geological history. During the Triassic period – roughly 250 million years ago – the present-day Balearic archipelago was flooded by the Mediterranean. The resulting sediment created sandstone and limestone deposits. These sedimentary rocks were then pushed to the surface during folding, and can still be seen in the central coastal area of the Serra de Tramuntana, Mallorca's northern mountain range. During the Paleocene period the Mediterranean grew narrower, and the mountain-building movements that resulted from the shift in the continental massifs gradually created the Serra de Tramuntana. The flatter regions of the island were then repeatedly flooded during the Tertiary period and alluvial deposits were formed.

During the Quaternary period, the sea level dropped temporarily and Mallorca and Menorca joined together to form one island, but were soon separated again. Mallorca's typical karst landscape is a remnant of the Ice Age: heavy rain perforated the limestone, creating crevices and furrows, and forming a large network of massive underground caverns and lakes. Several of these are in the southeastern hills, and sections have been made accessible to the public (*see pages 75–6 and 78*). Mallorca's sandy beaches are mainly made up of polished limestone and finely ground fragments of seashell and coral.

Landscape

Craggy cliffs of Port de Deià

The Serra de Tramuntana mountain range extends the entire length of Mallorca's northwest coast, from Andratx in the southwest to Pollença in the north. Without a doubt the most scenically impressive part of the island, it contains idyllic hiking routes and winding mountain roads. Deep ravines alternate with small gravel bays (Port de Valldemossa, Port de Deià, etc), though the only relatively large protected harbour is the one at Port de Sóller.

The 88-km (54-mile) long and 10–15-km (6–8-mile) wide mountain range has 10 main peaks, all of them over 1,000m (3,280ft). The highest is the Puig Major (1,445m/ 4,740ft) in the central part of the range, followed by Massanella (1,348m/4,422ft), Tomir (1,103m/3,618ft) and L'Ofre (1,091m/3,579ft). The Puig de Galatzó in the southern section of the chain also reaches an impressive height of 1,026m (3,360ft). The foothills of these northern mountains slope down gently towards Pollença before towering into bizarre rock formations yet again and falling steeply to the sea at Mallorca's northernmost point, the Cap de Formentor.

On the other side of the island lies the Serra de Levant. This eastern chain of hills is much gentler and more

Formentor

Cooling off in the sea

undulating than its serrated counterpart along the western coast with its steep cliffs. The highest elevations away from the actual coast are only just over 500m (1,640ft) or so, with the Puig de Son Morei near Artà reaching 561m (1,840ft). In the south of the island is the 543-m (1,781-ft) high table mountain, Puig de Randa.

The island's east coast has lots of tiny bays, or *calas*, along it, which are ideal for swimming or mooring yachts. Between the two mountain ranges is the broad, fertile, windmill-strewn plain known as the *pla*. This area between Muro and Sa Pobla is the bread basket of Mallorca; produce here is harvested up to four times a year.

Mallorca has no rivers to speak of apart from its many torrents, which swell rapidly after rain. Freshwater springs are found predominantly in the Serra de Tramuntana – there are several near Sóller – and the island also has two important reservoirs between Sóller and Lluc: Gorg Blau and Cúber. The most extensive area of marshland is the Parc Natural de La Albufera, between Alcúdia and Can Picafort, an important resting place for migratory birds on their travels between Africa and Europe. Other areas of marshland can be found around Pollença, and also at Es Salobrar near Colònia de Sant Jordi in the south.

Marshland grasses

7

Climate and when to go

The climate is subtropical Mediterranean, which means winter on Mallorca is milder than on mainland Spain. The high coastal mountain range also protects the island from much bad weather. Summers are dry and hot, winters mild but damp, and the temperature only very rarely falls below freezing point. November and April are the wettest months of the year, while hardly any rain falls during June, July and August.

Mallorca is a pleasant place to visit at any time of year, but the early months of spring are the most enjoyable. The

Deer at La Granja

Palma's Almudaina Palace

sea isn't quite warm enough for temperature-sensitive swimmers, but hiking holidays are ideal at this time. July and August tend to get very hot and the island is crowded with visitors. There can be quite a lot of rain between September and October, even causing temporary flooding, but conditions are still ideal for a hiking holiday and the sea is still fairly warm.

After Christmas the days are usually calm and mild and known as the *calmas* or *pequeño verano* 'little summer'. Almond-blossom time in early February is a real treat for hikers. The hotels open in winter all have central heating, and there are extensive programmes for winter guests.

Where to go

Mallorca has almost 200 beaches

Mallorca's holiday resort towns are on the coast, and the island has almost 200 beaches which would measure 50km (31 miles) if placed end to end. The longest sandy beaches are in the southwest along Palma Bay (Platja de Palma, Can Pastilla, S'Arenal), in the south near Colònia de Sant Jordi and in the northeast along the bays of Alcúdia and Pollença. Along the east coast, numerous bays cut sharply into the coastline (Cala Figuera), some of them full of pine trees (Cala Mondragó) or with picturesque harbours (Porto Colom, Cala d'Or, Porto Petro). The best part of the island for hikers is the mountain range in the northwest. Some mountain villages (Orient, Valldemossa, Fornalutx) offer cheap accommodation, and are ideal starting points for hikes lasting several days.

Flora and fauna

Palm trees in Palma

There is no need to go to a botanical garden or a nature reserve to appreciate Mallorca's many species of flora – they accompany you every step of the way. Country roads are lined with red poppies and yellow wild daisies and blue thistles grow in profusion in the meadows. The houses in the villages are adorned with geraniums, bougainvillaea and rock-roses; blue clematis often covers the ancient stone walls in the fields, and aromatic herbs such as rosemary and thyme grow wild in the hedgerows.

In the fertile valleys, sheltered from the wind, grow apricots, peaches and medlars – a fruit, like the carob tree, said to have been introduced by the Moors. The Spaniards introduced potatoes, maize and tomatoes. Citrus fruit in the area around Sóller is harvested two or three times a year (Mallorca's famously aromatic oranges are harvested once a year around the end of December). The olive trees and the fig trees on the terraces of the northwest coast are among the oldest Mediterranean flora. Above them, Aleppo pine can grow at altitudes as high as 700m (2,300ft), with holm oak even higher up.

Ancient olive tree in Deià

At the end of January, the blossom on Mallorca's six million almond trees turns large swathes of the island white, delighting hikers, photographers and artists alike. The carefully tended gardens on the country estates, with their cypresses, poplars and date palms, are another visual treat. Particularly magnificent are the gardens of the Alfàbia estate, originally laid out by the Moors, and the Botanicactus garden near Ses Salines, which is the largest botanical garden in Europe.

The magnificent gardens of Alfàbia

A gecko scurrying across a stone wall, or a lizard in the ivy, may provide a first encounter with the island's rich fauna. Hikers in the mountains are accompanied by the continual bleating of sheep and goats, and birds of prey – including the odd eagle – are often seen circling above the Serra de Tramuntana. There are ideal nesting conditions in the marshy area of the Albufera for wading birds, ducks, geese, frogs and turtles.

People and language

Over half of Mallorca's population of 629,000 live in Palma, the capital, while the rest are distributed across 53 municipal districts. In the peak season the population swells with tourists from all over the world and Spanish seasonal workers from the mainland. Most Mallorcans are of Catalan descent, and some families can trace their ancestry to Moorish-Catalan progenitors. There are Jewish and Italian minorities too, and several Mallorcans returned from France live in Sóller and speak French.

Time for a chat

Linguistically, Mallorca is part of Catalonia. The phrase *No soms Espanyols* 'We aren't Spanish', scrawled or painted on various flat surfaces, is an expression of the Mallorcans' fierce sense of independence from Spain's centralised government. During the second half of the 19th century the Castilian government had all the place-names on Mallorca systematically translated into Spanish, and during the Franco regime even speaking the Mallorcan dialect on the street could incur a prison sentence.

·The new constitution of 1978 accorded Spain's 17 autonomous regions cultural and linguistic independence; Catalan and the variation of it spoken on Mallorca, known as Mallorquí, were officially recognised. The children on the island are now learning their original language once again, and more Mallorquí is spoken on the streets these days than Castilian. Many Spanish road signs that were not switched quickly enough by the island's government have been repainted by the islanders themselves. The name for the main street in a village changed from Calle Mayor to Carrer Major; the word for airport, formerly *aeropuerto*, has now become *aeroport*, and signposts for the beach now say *platja* rather than *playa*.

Mallorquí bears many resemblances to Provençal French, and has some Arabic infusions. One of its idiosyncrasies is the use of the articles *en* (male) and *na* (female) before a person's Christian name. Road signs with the word *Son* (a contraction of *so*, meaning property or estate, and the article) are common, and can point the way to an estate (eg *Son Juan Jaume* = to Juan Jaume's estate) or to someone's house (eg *Can Amer* = The Amers' house).

There are several charming local proverbs and sayings on Mallorca. Many islanders justify the work they do for a living with the phrase: *Ens hem de guanyar les sopes* 'One has to earn one's daily bread'. Fishermen also have a popular slogan: *Qui vôl menjar peix es cul se hâ de banyar* 'He who wishes to eat fish must first wet his behind', while farmers retort: *Qui vôl es bessó que rompa sa mella* 'He who wishes to eat an almond must first break the shell'. The Mallorcans are industrious, but also very relaxed about work: *Tranquil!* 'Take it easy!' they say, because *Sâs coses atropelades no surteu acertades* 'Things done in haste tend not to succeed', and if something can't be managed straight away, then how about tomorrow? After all, *Hay més díes que llonganisses* 'There are more days than sausages'.

Economy

The fertile Pla de Mallorca in the middle of the island has been in agricultural use since time immemorial. Many landlords have left the administration of their property to tenant farmers (*amos*), who look after it together with labourers (*missatjes*). Agriculture is not as profitable today as it once was, and several landlords have increased their income by either working in the construction business, or letting out individual houses or outbuildings to tourists. Pig farming is a very old tradition, though, and the varieties of Mallorcan pork sausage known as *Sobrassada*, *Botifarró* and *Llonganissa* are justly famed.

10

Catching up with the news

A traditional pig

Mallorcan and Spanish flags

11

Other leading export articles are herbal liqueurs, almonds and potatoes. Mass tourism has radically altered the island's infrastructure and in just 30 years its predominantly agrarian economy has become a service economy, with tourism accounting for a full two-thirds of the island's gross domestic product. This has resulted in a demand for extra labour, especially during the peak season. Most of the workers come from mainland Spain and around 13,000 settled on the island during the 1960s and 70s. The 1980s saw the arrival of seasonal workers from Andalusia. Many of these so-called *forasters* (outsiders) are re-hired each summer by the same employers.

Leather is the most important cottage industry on Mallorca. Numerous factories around the town of Inca produce leather goods and shoes which are then sold in mainland Spain and also exported abroad.

Despite its island status, fishing does not play a significant role. Seafood often needs to be imported from mainland Spain to keep pace with demand.

Leather goods at Inca market

Politics and administration

The new Spanish constitution passed on 29 December 1978 made Spain a collection of 17 autonomous regions. Politically, Mallorca is a member of the Balearic Islands which form a *Comunidad autónoma* within the Spanish state. They were one of the last regions to be granted autonomy (in 1983), mainly because of differences of opinion among the various islands. The first local parliamentary elections were held in May 1983. All the islands together form a Spanish province, with Palma as the capital. The city is also the province's ecclesiastical, military and judicial headquarters. Mallorca is made up of five main administrative regions (Tramuntana, Raiguer, Es Pla, Migjorn and Llevant), subdivided into 53 municipal districts.

Parliament building in Palma

Historical Highlights

6000–4000BC Palaeolithic period. Earliest traces of human habitation. Burial chambers.

2000–1300BC Pre-Talayotic period. Elongated graves known as *navetas* are built, as well as rock-cut tombs and burial caves.

1300–123BC Talayotic period. Chambered towers of stone known as *talayots* are built in great numbers across Mallorca, sometimes situated inside villages with Cyclopean walls (eg Ses Païses, near Artà). The Balearic Islands are situated on the great trading routes that crisscross the Mediterranean Sea and there is active trade with the Phoenicians, Carthaginians and Greeks. Classical texts refer to Mallorcan *honderos* (stone slingers) fighting for the Carthaginians in the famous Punic wars.

123BC The Romans arrive, under the leadership of Quintus Caecilius Metellus. Mallorca becomes part of the Roman Empire.

1st–5th century AD The island flourishes under Roman rule. The towns of Pollentia (the powerful) and Palmaria (the symbol of victory) are founded. Olive cultivation, viniculture and salt-mining are introduced. Roads, temples and theatres are built. The remains of the Roman theatre at Alcúdia and the Roman bridge near Pollença date from this time.

AD426 Mallorca conquered for the first time by the Vandal leader Gunderico.

465 The island is finally subdued by Gunderico's brother, Genserico, who incorporates Mallorca into the Vandal Empire. Christians are persecuted.

534 Mallorca is conquered by Byzantium, and ruled by Justinian as part of the province of Sardinia. Christianity is restored to the island and Early Christian basilicas constructed (eg Son Fiol, near Santa Maria).

From 707 Moorish pirates make a number of attempts to conquer the island.

902 Mallorca is conquered by the Caliphate of Córdoba.

902–1229 The island flourishes under Moorish rule. The Moors improve agriculture and irrigation (windmills and waterwheels introduced) and develop its crafts and commerce. Roman Pollentia is rebuilt, renamed Alcúdia, and made the capital; Palma becomes Medina Mayurka. The Almudaina Palace is built, along with several castles and fortresses (Alaró, Castell del Rei). The Moors' contribution to the island's folklore, language and cuisine is still evident today.

1015 Mallorca is annexed to another Moslem 'kingdom', the 'Taifa of Denia'.

1087–1114 Mallorca is an independent *taifa*.

1114 A group of Pisa-Catalans try to conquer the islands of Eivissa and Mallorca. The siege of Palma lasts eight months. After the city is defeated and sacked, the invaders go home.

1115–1203 The Almorávides, a tribe from North Africa, arrive to help the Mallorcan Moslems and stay on to occupy the island. The island experiences a renewed period of prosperity. The Almorávides' dominion extends extends as far as Tunisia and Tripolitania.

1203–29 The Baleares fall into the hands of Almohadian tribes from Algeria and Denia. Political instability allows the reconquest of Mallorca by the Catalans.

1229 Tired of the Mallorcan Moors plundering Catalan boats, James I of Aragon (the Conqueror) launches an invasion of the island with 15,000 men and 1,500 horses. After three months of fierce fighting the island is conquered and annexed to Aragon.

1235–1315 Life of the prestigious Mallorcan philosopher, mystic and scientist, Ramón Llull.

1276 After the death of James I, the kingdom of Aragon is divided up among his sons. The newly created Kingdom of Mallorca is entrusted to James II.

1285 First expedition by the Catalans to recover the Kingdom of Mallorca by force. A later expedition is abandoned by order of the pope.

1312–24 Reign of King Sanç, son of King James II of Mallorca.

1324–44 Reign of King James III of Mallorca, bringing with it a period of great economic prosperity which sees the flowering of the island's agriculture, industry and navigation. New villages are founded, Bellver Castle is built, the Almudiana is transformed into a splendid Gothic palace and work starts on the building of the Convent of Sant Francesc. Palma becomes one of the richest cities in the Mediterranean.

1344 Unhappy about Mallorca's independent successes, Pedro IV of Aragon launches an invasion and reincorporates the Baleares into the Kingdom of Aragon.

1349 James III, the third and last king of Mallorca, tries to recover the Kingdom of Mallorca, but is killed at the battle of Llucmajor by his relative, Pedro IV.

1479 Kingdom of España formed by uniting the Kingdom of Castile and the Kingdom of Aragon, including Mallorca.

16th century A series of uprisings caused by popular discontent against the nobility.

1554 Palma is fortified to protect it from attacks by Turkish and Moorish pirates.

1700 The War of the Spanish Succession begins with the accession to the throne of Felipe V. Mallorca's state of semi-autonomy allowed by the Habsburgs is over.

1715 Troops loyal to Felipe V disembark at Mallorca. The Grand and General Council is replaced by an 'Audience' supervised by the Captain General of the King's troops, and the use of Castilian (the Spanish language) is made obligatory for all public and official transactions.

1713–84 Life and times of Fray Junípero Serra, founder of the missions of California, including San Francisco.

1785 Treaty of Algiers is signed, ending piracy while establishing the Mallorcan 'corsairs' who are given permission by the king to 'defend' their homeland. The most famous of these corsairs is Captain Antoni Barceló, who writes himself into the history books by becoming Lieutenant General of the Spanish Armada.

1803–13 The War of Independence against the invading troops of Napoleon. Many refugees arrive on Mallorca, provoking social and political unrest among the islanders.

1820–22 Massive emigration to Algeria and South America.

1837 Establishment of the first regular steamship service between Mallorca and the Iberian Peninsula.

1879–98 The years of the 'gold fever'. Period of social and commercial splendour through wine and almond trade. This comes to an abrupt end with the arrival of the *phylloxera* virus, which destroys the booming wine industry on the islands, and the loss of Spain's last colonies. Economic decline results in waves of emigration to the mainland and America.

1936 The leftist parties belonging to the so-called People's Front win the parliamentary elections (16 February). The rightist leader Calvo Sotelo is assassinated on 13 July. This sparks off the uprising under General Francisco Franco on 16 July, which soon spreads across Spain.

1939 Barcelona conquered by the Nationalists on 16 January, followed by Madrid on 30 March. The Civil War ends on 1 April.

1947 Plebiscite held about restoring the monarchy. Franco remains head of state.

1960 Mallorca's airport is built. Tourism begins to replace agriculture as the island's main source of income.

1975 Juan Carlos ascends the throne after Franco's death.

1978 Spain receives a democratic constitution.

1979 The Balearic Islands become an autonomous region, and the Mallorcan language is officially recognised.

1982 Spain becomes a member of NATO.

1986 Spain joins the EC.

Palma Cathedral

Preceding pages: Port de Sóller

Route 1

★★★ **Palma de Mallorca** *See map on page 18*

History

Over half the population of Mallorca live in the island's capital Palma, known locally as *la ciutat*, 'the city'. It lies on the southwestern coast of the Bay of Mallorca in the centre of the island of Palma, which is 16km (10 miles) wide. The name Palma derives from the old Roman name for the town, Palmaria (victory palm). It was founded by them above the ruins of a talayotic settlement, on the site of today's cathedral and Royal Palace. In 902 the Moors conquered the island and turned Palma into Medina Mayurka, a city full of mosques, bath-houses and gardens, easily on a par with Seville, Córdoba and Toledo.

The capital was first fortified under Wali Mobaxir (1093–1114), but that didn't stop King James I winning back the island for Christendom at the beginning of the 13th century. The Christians landed at Santa Ponça on the south coast in 1229, and the last Moorish wali, Abú Yahya, sought refuge in the walled city. After a three-month siege, the king's troops finally took Medina Mayurka, and renamed it Ciutat de Mallorca. The Moorish city wall was strengthened still further, and the mosques were turned into Christian churches. The foundation stone for Palma Cathedral was laid at the behest of King James I, and his son James II built Bellver Castle.

Busy Mediterranean trade necessitated the construction of the Consolat de Mar (Consulate of the Sea) in 1325 (*see page 26*). Palma then developed into an important international harbour and also became a leading centre of cartography – Mallorcan maps were not only works of art, but also models of precision. Many were the work of the

The city wall

The marina

island's Jewish population. Persecution of the Jews began at the end of the 14th century when the Xuetes (Mallorcan Jews) were forcibly baptised and compelled to live in the Call (Palma's Jewish Quarter). The Inquisition arrived in 1431, and the resulting fanaticism culminated in the gruesome *Fogó dels Jueus* (Burning of the Jews) in 1691.

Meanwhile, pirates were becoming more and more troublesome, and in 1575 the Italian engineer Jacobo Paleario was entrusted with building new fortifications. The last section was completed in 1801, only to be torn down again 100 years later when the *avenidas* (broad avenues) were built, which today keep much of the traffic away from the city centre.

During the Middle Ages the sea extended as far as the site of today's Teatre Principal, where the mouth of the Riera river once was. It kept overflowing its banks, and 5,000 people were drowned during a severe flood in 1403. The river was then re-routed around the city centre in 1613. The first regular ferry link between Palma and the Spanish mainland was opened in 1837, and in 1875 the first railway on the island (Palma–Inca) was officially inaugurated. In 1900 Palma had just 64,000 inhabitants; by 1940 the figure had risen to 115,000, and today the city's population numbers around 300,000. Palma is the seat of government for the autonomous community of the Balearic Islands and the archipelago's cultural centre.

City Tour 1: the Portella Quarter

At the centre of Palma, on the Plaça de la Almoina, the cathedral and the Royal Palace stand opposite one another. Palma's ★★★ **Cathedral ❶**, known to locals as *La Seu*, was built in the Gothic style on the site of the main Moorish mosque, which King James I pulled down. The foundation stone for the new church was laid in 1230, and construction work continued until the west portal was completed in 1604. A severe earthquake in 1851 damaged several parts of the cathedral, but by 1904 it had been thoroughly renovated (fortunately with no loss of its original character).

Cathedral buttresses

The golden-brown sandstone exterior of this massive Gothic church has two fine portals, both of them always kept closed: the ★★ **Puerta del Mirador** is the southern one facing the sea, built between 1380 and 1420, and on the south side is the ★ **main portal** (1594), with the rose window above it. The vault of the three-aisled, 121-m (396-ft) long interior is supported by 14 elegant, 21-m (68-ft) high pillars. The largest of the cathedral's seven rose windows – the so-called ★★ **Queen of Rose Windows** – is world-famous. It is 12m (42ft) across and composed of 1,236 separate sections of stained glass. The cathedral is also known as the 'Cathedral of Light', because of the

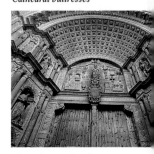

The main portal and rose window detail

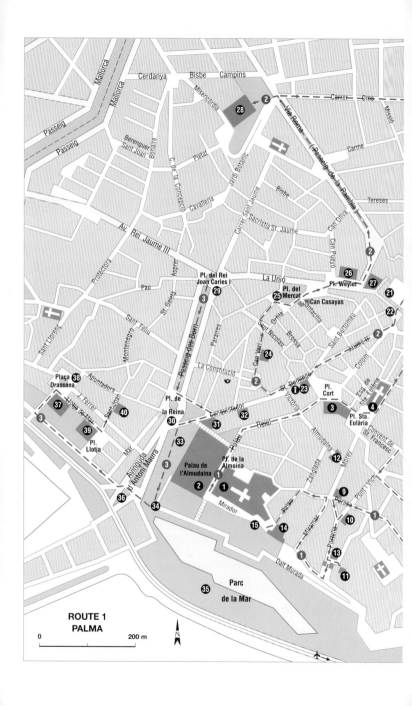

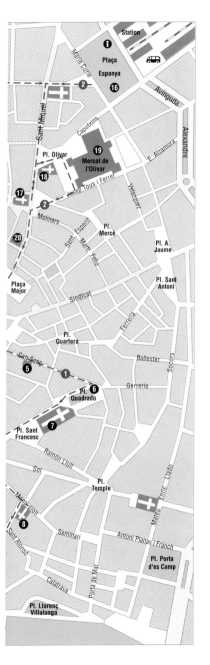

Sights

1. Palma Cathedral
2. Almudaina Palace
3. Town Hall
4. Church of Santa Eulàlia
5. Can Joan de S'Aigo
6. Plaça Quadrado
7. Monastery of Sant Francesc
8. Monti-Sion Jesuit Church
9. Casa Oleza
10. Mallorca Museum
11. Arab Baths
12. Arc de l'Almudaina
13. Palau Formiguera
14. Diocesan Museum
15. Mirador de la Catedral
16. Plaça Espanya
17. Church of Sant Miquel
18. Church of Sant Antoni
19. Mercat de l'Olivar
20. Collecció March
21. Plaça Major
22. Plaça Marquès del Palmer
23. Can Corbella
24. Palau Pelaires
25. Plaça dei Mercat
26. Gran Hotel
27. Teatre Principal
28. Casa de la Misericòrdia
29. Plaça del Rei Joan Carles I
30. Plaça de la Reina
31. Barthomeu March Library
32. Parliament Building
33. S'Hort del Rei
34. Arch of Drassanes
35. Parc de la Mar
36. Ramón Llull memorial
37. Consulate of the Sea
38. Plaça Drassana
39. La Llotja
40. Abaco Palace

brilliant effects whenever the morning sun shines directly through the rose windows.

The tombs of Mallorcan kings James II and III in the Capilla Trinidad at the east end are the work of Catalan sculptor Frederic Marès. The new chapter house contains several fine treasures, including a 16th-century monstrance by Jaume Nicolau. Outside the Casa de l'Almoina, which houses the **Cathedral Museum**, sections of the original Roman city can be observed through the glass floor.

Opposite the cathedral, the ★★**Almudaina Palace** (Palau de l'Almudaina) ❷ dates from the Moorish occupation. Originally the seat of the Moorish viziers, it was used during the Middle Ages as a royal residence by the kings of Aragon and Mallorca before becoming the headquarters of the captain-general. Today this is where King Juan Carlos holds his audiences. The pretty royal courtyard (Patio del Rey) was laid out in 1309, and is surrounded by fine arcades; the magnificent **throne room** and the Gothic **chapel of Santa Anna** are also well worth visiting (Monday to Friday 10am–2pm and 4–6pm; during the summer 10am–6pm, Saturday 10am–2pm; conducted tours).

Go along the Carrer del Palau Reial now to the Plaça del Cort, dominated by the magnificent Renaissance and baroque facade of the ★**Town Hall** (Ajuntament) ❸. The massive roof supported by 11 beams in the form of male and female figures is most impressive. Inside there are several valuable paintings, including a San Sebastián attributed to Van Dyck and *The Execution of Cabrit and Bassa* by Joan Bestard. The building also contains the archives of the old Kingdom of Mallorca. The nearby church of ★**Santa Eulàlia** ❹ was built at the beginning of the 15th century, and contains altar paintings by Francisco Gomez. Students and government officials congregate at the Café

Almudaina Palace and guard

Moderno in the square in front of the church. Behind the church in the dark Carrer Sanç is the **Can Joan de S'Aigo** , the chocolate shop where the artist Joan Miró used to indulge in his hot chocolate and almond cake.

Nearby lies the **Plaça Quadrado** ❻, with its three-storeyed **Can Barcelo building**, constructed at the turn of the century. The facade is decorated with oriel windows and has several delightful mosaics portraying women going about their daily chores.

The ★★ **monastery of Sant Francesc** ❼ was founded by James I in 1232, and its single-aisled Gothic church dates from the end of the 13th century. It was built by the Franciscan Order on the foundations of a mosque, and is notable for its baroque facade, with an equestrian statue of St George and Plateresque rose window. The Late Gothic cloister with its slender columns dates from the 14th century, and is one of the largest of its kind. The monastery church is the last resting place of the Catalan scholar and mystic Ramón Llull (1235–1316), who travelled through North Africa and Asia Minor trying to convert Muslims to Christianity. The sculpture group outside the building depicts another famous missionary born in Mallorca, Fray Junípero Serra, the founder of San Francisco (*see page 79*), seen here with an Indian boy.

Monastery of Sant Francesc

21

Cross the former Jewish quarter and the ★ **Monti-Sion Jesuit Church** ❽ comes into view. It was built on the ruins of a synagogue in the 17th century and has a magnificent baroque portal.

Fray Junípero Serra

Palma's 'palace quarter' lies between the churches of Santa Eulàlia, Sant Francesc and the former city gate of La Portella. Dignified facades conceal huge patios with spacious entrance halls, and inquisitive passers-by can often glimpse some very fine architecture inside. One of the best examples is the **Casa Oleza** ❾ in the Carrer Morey, with its pebbled patio surrounded by arcades and a Renaissance stairway leading to the first floor. At Carrer Portella 5 is the 17th-century palazzo Ca La Gran Cristiana (also known as Palau Aiamans or Can Villalonga-Desbrull), housing the ★★ **Mallorca Museum** (Museu de Mallorca) ❿ (10am–2pm and 4–7pm, closed Sunday afternoon and Monday). Several thousand exhibits from various epochs make this museum, founded in 1961, one of the most important on the island. They include many archaeological finds from Talayotic and Roman times, a collection of Moorish ceramics, and also several paintings and altar-pieces dating from the 14th to 19th centuries.

Casa Oleza

The ★★ **Arab Baths** (Banys Arabs) ⓫ (Carrer Serra 7) date from the 10th century and are almost all that remains of the Moorish city of Medina Mayurka apart from the Arch of Drassanes in the royal park (*see page 25*). The

Inside the Arab baths

baths probably formed part of a Moorish palace. By contrast, the ★ **Arc de l'Almudaina** ⑫ in the street of the same name is a relic of the Roman fortifications, and was later incorporated into the wall of the Moorish city.

Next to the Arab Baths is the **Palau Formiguera** ⑬, where the Archduke Ludwig Salvator (*see page 38*) stayed during his second visit to the island in 1871. The episcopal palace behind the cathedral houses the ★★ **Diocesan Museum** ⑭ (Museo Diocesà, closed for renovation). The collection includes Mallorcan medieval paintings, wooden statues of the Virgin, altarpieces (including the celebrated retable of Sant Jordi, with a view of Palma as it looked in the 15th century by Pere Niçard), a coin collection and ceramics. The most unusual exhibit is the *Drac de Na Còca*, a small embalmed crocodile; it lived in the sewers of the Portella Quarter during the 17th century and terrorised the populace. A version in stone can be admired on the roof of the Can Enric España, opposite the museum.

Directly next to the episcopal palace, on the side of the cathedral facing the sea, is what remains of the old city wall, now known as **Mirador de la Catedral** ⑮. This observation point (there are several coin-operated telescopes) affords a fine view across the calm water of the Parc de la Mar, with its mural by Joan Miró, and the Gulf of Palma.

22

City Tour 2: The heart of Palma

Statue of James I

Bus and train passengers all arrive at Palma's busy **Plaça Espanya** ⑯. Walk downhill from here past the equestrian statue of **King James I**, and then turn left into the Carrer Sant Miquel (there's a good old-fashioned coffee-house in this shopping street called Moka). On the right is the church of **Sant Miquel** ⑰, which was also built on the site of a mosque. The first Christian Mass after the conquest was celebrated in this church, and one of the side-chapels contains the Verge de la Salut, which is supposed to have accompanied James I on his journey from the mainland. In 1979 the Basque bank BBV restored the oval cloister which used to belong to the church of **Sant Antoni** ⑱ and the adjoining hospice (1768), and it now has an exhibition hall (Carrer Sant Miquel 30). On the left is

Fruit stall at Mercat de l'Olivar

the imposing cast-iron construction housing the ★**Mercat de l'Olivar** ⑲, the city's largest market. Alongside the huge variety of fruit, vegetables, fish, cheese and sausage, there are also many *tapas* stands (*see page 89*).

At Sant Miquel 11, just before the arcades of the Plaça Major come into view, there is a palace containing the ★★ **Collecció March** ⑳, a banking family's collection of 57 paintings including works by Pablo Picasso, Antoni Tàpies and Miguel Barceló. From **Plaça Major** ㉑ a large archway leads to the neighbouring **Plaça Marquès** del Palmer ㉒ with its two fine art nouveau buildings, ★ L'Aguila and ★ Can Fortesa-Rei. Another attractive art nouveau building is the ★ Can Corbella ㉓, Carrer Santo Domingo 1, built by Nicolau Lliteres at the end of the 19th century. The windows are decorated in neo-Mudejar style, and the roof is adorned with an octagonal tower.

In the Carrer Jaume II, the La Montana sausage shop with its wares dangling outside is popular with photographers, as is the grocery shop called Colmado Santo Domingo (Carrer Santo Domingo 3). The boutiques in the Carrer Verí have the very latest fashions, and there are also several galleries of modern art. The **Palau Pelaires** ㉔ (Carrer Verí 5), in particular, contains an important collection of contemporary paintings, and has alternating exhibitions on varying themes. Directly next door to it, at Carrer Verí 7 (first floor), is the Galerie Joan Guaita and the Escuela Libre de Mediteráneo school of art, founded by the Catalan painter Xim Torrent Lladó. Shortly after his death in 1984, a large exhibition was held in his honour in the Llotja (*see page 26*).

Those with a sweet tooth should definitely drop into the La Pajarita chocolate shop at Carrer Sant Nicolau 3; it was founded in 1872 and has a magnificent display window. A few steps further on, the narrow streets emerge into the attractive **Plaça del Mercat** ㉕. It's no longer a market square, but the film-director-style chairs at the Cine Café are a good place to take a break and admire the magnificent art nouveau buildings. The two sections of the ★ **Can Casayas**, built between 1908 and 1911 by the architects Fracesca Roca and Guillem Reynés, are separated by the Carrer Santacilia. One half until recently housed the Hostal Menorquina, but an insurance company has now moved into the restored building. The two sections, with their undulating facades and irregular windows, are reminiscent of the style of Catalan architect Antoni Gaudí. The art nouveau facade of the ★ **Forn d'Es Teatre** is a few steps away – the smell of freshly baked bread in the early morning is irresistible.

Treat yourself   **23**

Can Casayas

The Gran Hotel

Directly opposite, on the Plaça Weyler, is one of Palma's finest buildings, the ★★★ **Gran Hotel** ㉖ (daily except Monday 10am–9pm, Sunday 10am–2pm). Today it houses an arts centre sponsored by the La Caixa savings bank. The Gran Hotel was not only the first modern hotel on the island but also a very popular meeting place for intellectuals and artists at the turn of the century. It was designed by the Catalan architect Lluís Domènech i Montaner (1850–1923), a leading exponent of Modernisme. The building remained a hotel until the outbreak of the Spanish Civil War (1936–39), but then it fell into disrepair. Restoration was completed in 1993, and a look inside is an absolute must for any visitor to Palma. On three

Flower stall on the Rambla

Teatre Principal

Bar Bosch

storeys, original furniture of the hotel can be admired alongside large-scale landscapes by Catalan artists Santiago Rusinyol and Joaquim Mir, and also sculpture by Eusebi Arnau. The first floor includes the most representative work of the Catalan painter Hermen Anglada Camarasa (1872–1959); the second and third floors contain smaller oil paintings and over 100 sketches by the artist. There is a bookshop and a concert hall, and the café is an 'in' place to meet.

The rather stern-looking facade on the opposite side of the street belongs to the magnificent ★ **Teatre Principal** ㉗, modelled after the Liceu opera house in Barcelona. The Via Roma, an attractive leafy avenue and a popular place for a stroll, is just around the corner. Its resemblance to the main shopping street in Barcelona has led many to refer to it as Palma's Rambla, and it actually follows the course of the river that ran through the centre of the city before it was diverted in the 17th century. At the end of the Rambla on the left is the **Casa de la Misericòrdia** ㉘, a former Jesuit almshouse which was redesigned in the neoclassical style in the mid-19th century. Today it belongs to the Consell Insular, housing the conservatory of music and dance and various libraries.

The **botanical gardens** next door with their interesting Spanish contemporary sculpture are a good place to relax before returning via the Carrer Oms to the Plaça Espanya.

City Tour 3: The city by the sea

A stroll through the section of Palma that faces the sea is still relaxing, despite the rumble of passing traffic. At the junction of the shopping street Avinguda Rei Jaume III and the Carrer La Unió is the **Plaça del Rei Joan Carles I** ㉙. From its famous Bar Bosch there's a good view of the **Turtle Fountain**, so named because of the four turtles supporting its obelisk. The Passeig des Born begins here, a tree-lined avenue where jousting tournaments were held during medieval times. On the right is the impressive ★★ **Palau Solleric**, one of the finest palaces in Palma with its wrought-iron gate and attractively painted facade. It re-opened in April 1995 and houses exhibitions of contemporary art.

There are two stone sphinxes shaded by massive trees at the junction of the Passeig with the **Plaça de la Reina** ⑳. On the left-hand side of this square, at the foot of the flight of steps leading up to the cathedral, there is a leafy little park with palm trees, cypresses and stone benches, guarded by lion's-head gargoyles spouting water. The Palau March on the corner above this park contains the ★ **Barthomeu March Library** ㉛, an extensive collection of documents on Balearic themes. Next door is the magnificent ★★ **Parliament Building** ㉜, formerly the headquarters of the elitist Circulo Artístic Mallorquí.

Sphinx at Plaça de la Reina

Every day, on the corner of the ★★ **S'Hort del Rei** ㉝, the former royal park, hundreds of passers-by stick their heads through the opening in the Miró sculpture *Personatge*, known familiarly as 'The Egg'. At the entrance to the park is a gnarled olive tree, and a plaque stands in memory of the Teatro Lírico which stood on this site from 1902 to 1967. Directly opposite, on the other side of the Avinguda d'Antoni Maura, is the Café Lírico, one of the city's traditional coffee-houses. The fountain at the centre of the park is reminiscent of the Arab Gardens in Granada, and the hum of the traffic is suddenly very distant in this oasis of tranquillity. A short distance from the fountain is the statue of the Balearic Slinger (*see page 86*). Green gates lead to a small pond with swans, situated beneath the high city walls. Above the pond is the ★ **Arch of Drassanes** (Arc de la Drassana Musulmana) ㉞, an archway dating from the Moorish occupation; it used to lead to the shipyard and to the walls' hidden harbour.

25

Miró's 'Egg'

The high city walls and the towers of the cathedral can be seen reflected in the calm waters of the **Parc de la Mar** ㉟; at the head of this small lake is a modern piece of sculpture that is supposed to represent the discovery of America. The memorial to the Catalan scholar and mystic **Ramón Llull** ㊱ (1235–1316) can be seen on the traffic island between the Avinguda d'Antoni Maura and the Passeig de Sagrera. The palm-lined harbour promenade leads on to the fishing harbour, past a monumental sundial showing the signs of the zodiac. Between the fishing harbour on the Moll de Sant Pere and the Real Club Náutico (a yacht club with access for members only), at the point where the Riera reaches the sea, is the attractive little **chapel of Sant Telm**.

The palm-lined promenade

La Llotja and the 17th-century Consulate of the Sea

Below the Baluarte de Sant Pere, an impressive section of city wall, is the ★ **Consulate of the Sea** (Consolat del Mar) **37**. This 17th-century Renaissance building, with its fine loggia, was where disputes among the powerful trading fleets were regularly settled. Today it is the seat of the autonomous government of the Balearic Islands. To the rear is the tranquil **Plaça Drassana 38**, with its monument to the geographer and mariner Jaume Ferrer who sailed from Mallorca to Senegal in the 14th century. The park between the Consolat del Mar and the Llotja is bordered by the Porta del Mar, a former city gate.

The real highlight of this tour is a visit to ★★★ **La Llotja 39**, the former exchange, and a symbol of Mallorca's role in Mediterranean trade. It is a superb example of the Spanish Gothic style; the emperor Charles V thought that the Llotja was actually a church because of its elegant form. It was designed by Guillem Sagrera (1380–1454), and built between 1426 and 1451. The battlemented building has a magnificent portal, with the Gothic figure of the Angel de la Mercadería at its centre. The interior, now used as an exhibition hall, is spanned by ribbed vaulting supported by six slender spiral columns reminiscent of palm trees. Outside is a palm-lined square with cafés and restaurants; the nearby Carrer Llotja de Mar contains typical residential buildings with wrought-iron balconies and oriel windows. A good place to go for a meal in this street is the old Café Sa Llotja at No 2.

Inside the Abaco

Nearby, in the Carrer Sant Joan, the ancient palace known as the ★★ **Abaco 40** is also well worth a visit. Passing through the heavy wooden door is like stepping into another world entirely, full of soft brocade, incense, antique furniture, flickering candelabra and baroque music.

Outside the centre

Those leaving the centre of Palma and going beyond the Passeig de Mallorca and the Riera will discover several fine sights, including the ★★ **Poble Espanyol** (Carrer Poble Espanyol 39), the city's 'Spanish village', with its collection of Spanish buildings dating from different epochs. The houses, all faithful copies of originals, contain cafés, restaurants and craft workshops.

Poble Espanyol

Above the part of the city known as El Terreno (popular with many artists and intellectuals at the end of the 19th century, including Bernard Shaw, Gertrude Stein and Camilo José Cela), 112m (367ft) above the sea and surrounded by pine trees, is ★★ **Bellver Castle**. To reach the castle hill, go up the Carrer Bellver from the Plaça Gomila and then walk through a brief stretch of pine forest. Bellver Castle is the only round castle in all of Spain. It was commissioned by James II from the architect Pere Salvà, and completed in 1311. The ramparts, moat and watchtowers were added later on. The castle served as a summer residence for the kings of Mallorca, and later became a political prison. The dungeon beneath the 33-m (108-ft) high Torre de Homenaje known as the *Olla* 'the pot' was particularly feared. The keep is connected by a bridge to the castle, and the inner courtyard with its fountain is surrounded by a two-storey loggia.

The castle now contains the **Museum of Municipal History**, with exhibits from Moorish and Roman times (castle and museum Monday to Sunday 8am–6pm; museum closed Sunday). The most compelling feature, though, is the ★★ **view** from the top, considered the best in the city.

The view from the castle

The ★ **Miró Foundation** (Fundació Miró, Carrer Joan de Saridakis 29, Tuesday to Saturday 10am–7pm, winter 10am–6pm, Sunday 10am–3pm) lies in the suburb of Cala Major above the Marivent Palace, the Spanish royal family's summer residence. The sculptor and painter Joan Miró was born in 1883, and lived on Mallorca from 1956 until his death in 1983. His 17th-century house, San Boter, high above Palma Bay, has formed part of the Miró Foundation since 1992. Paintings, drawings and many personal documents are on display. Part of the collection is housed in the new exhibition complex, designed by the Spanish architect Rafael Moneo. The Son Abrines studio, situated behind the main building, with its shiny white walls and blue, red and yellow doors, is named Taller Sert after Miró's friend and house architect. The interior of the studio contains half-finished works, easels, brushes, rolls of paper and sketches, giving the impression that Miró might return to his canvas at any moment. The art centre also includes a library, a newspaper archive, a bookshop, a souvenir shop and a cafeteria.

Miró miracle

Route 2

Idyllic coastlines and magnificent mountain scenery

**Peguera – Port d'Andratx – (Sant Elm) – Andratx –
Estallencs – Banyalbufar – La Granja – Galilea –
Peguera (85km/52 miles)**

The southwestern coast of Mallorca, between Palma and
Peguera, is densely populated and completely taken up by
tourism. Things start getting picturesque only in the bay
of Camp de Mar, where the coast road winds its way
through forests as far as Port d'Andratx. There's a good
detour at this point to the small bathing resort of Sant Elm,
with its famous Dragon Island. The route then continues
onwards from the small town of Andratx across the southern reaches of the Serra de Tramuntana, up the slopes of
the 1,026-m (3,360-ft) high Galatzó and around numerous hairpins to the coast. The two pretty towns of Estallencs and Banyalbufar are artists' colonies. The highlight

La Granja   of the route is a visit to the country estate of La Granja,

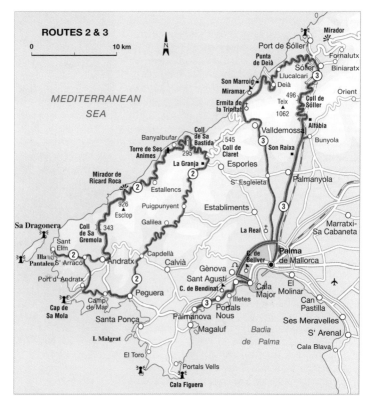

Peguera bay

with its wonderfully restored manor house and attractive park. Another series of bends, along minor roads this time, leads across scenic mountain landscape to the remote mountain village of Galilea, and then back to Peguera.

Peguera, the starting point for this route, belongs to the municipal district of Calvià, which has grown extremely rich on tourism. Much has been done to improve the local infrastructure in recent years. The new motorway between Palma and Andratx has kept a lot of traffic away from Peguera and Palmira Beach has also been artificially extended. Peguera, with its discos, restaurants and souvenir shops, is a particularly popular destination for German visitors to the island.

Leave Peguera in the direction of Camp de Mar and follow a turn-off down to the **Bay of Fornells**, where the holiday homes are built around the coast like an amphitheatre. The original architecture here is the work of Pedro Ozoup, who was born in Russia and studied architecture in Berlin.

Between Peguera and Camp de Mar is the rocky **Cap Andritxol**, a 184-ha (450-acre) large nature reserve with a watchtower dating from 1850.

The country road now leads through shady pine forests to the neighbouring resort of Camp de Mar, and then around a series of bends along the coast as far as ★ **Port d'Andratx**, with its pretty harbour full of fishing boats and elegant yachts. Above the harbour is the town's small fortified church. The lighthouse lies 3km (1¾ miles) away on the **Cap de Sa Mola**, and can be reached by road. On clear days the island of Ibiza can be seen from the top.

The small town of Andratx lies 5km (3 miles) inland, but just beforehand it's worth taking a short detour via ★★ **S'Arracó**. This idyllic little village lies at the centre of the Palomera Valley, which was uninhabited until the

29

Pretty harbour at Port d'Andratx

The beach at Sant Elm

Sa Dragonera

17th century. The church of Sant Crist contains the marble statue of Nostra Senyora de Sa Trapa, brought here by French Trappist monks in the 18th century. The old well on the Plaça de Toledo has been converted into a pretty fountain and the Sarracotta store on the main road through the village has good glassware.

At this point it is worth dropping down to the rather remote coastal village of ★★ **Sant Elm** (San Telmo) at the westernmost point of the island. It has only recently been discovered by the tourist trade and although a few apartment blocks have sprung up on the edge of the village, the beach, situated beneath the ruins of an old castle, is still peaceful. There's no local supply of drinking water (it arrives by lorry), and the few hotels and restaurants are closed in winter.

The terraces of the seafood restaurant at the end of the village are the best place from which to admire the rocky, almost sinister-looking island of ★ **Sa Dragonera** just off the coast, crowned by an ancient look-out tower. Once the haunt of smugglers, today it is a nature reserve. Trips across to 'Dragon Island' can be organised via Cruceros Margarita; the boat leaves from the restaurant terrace mentioned above. The area around Sant Elm is also popular with divers and yachtsmen.

One fascinating hiking destination from Sant Elm is the ruined Trappist monastery of ★★ **Sa Trapa**, a refuge for the monks forced to flee France after the Revolution. The monastery was secularised under Isabella II in 1835, and today it belongs to the GOB environmental protection group. The walking tour takes roughly four hours, and passes through some magnificent coastal scenery, with maquis, Aleppo pine and lots of fine views of Sa Dragonera. The 16th-century watchtower in the bay of Cala Basset on the way can be climbed.

Back at S'Arracó the road continues over the Coll de S'Arracó to arrive at **Andratx** (pop. 7,000). This little town lies at the centre of a fertile agricultural region. Construction work began on its church after Mallorca was recaptured by the Christians in 1229, and the building served to protect the local population from several pirate raids (the bloodiest of which occurred between 1551 and 1553). Many of the buildings surrounding the church date from the last century and were built by migrants who returned from the Caribbean. Although the land around Andratx has been famous since antiquity for having plenty of water, it was only connected to the main supply in 1993. Above the town is the estate of **Son Mas**, originally a Moorish fortress (closed to visitors), and also the fine old cemetery.

The route continues past Andratx and up the Coll de Sa Gremola (343m/1,125ft) as far as the steep cliffs along the coast. The road then carries on high above the sea as far as ★★ **Mirador de Ricardo Roca**, an observation point above a tunnel with fantastic views across the blue sea, with the rough cliffs of the Punta de Na Forada to the south and the Punta de Son Serralta to the north.

Mirador de Ricardo Roca

The pine-shaded road (widened in 1994) continues onward to **Estallencs**, a sleepy little village on the slopes of the 1,026-m (3,360-ft) high **Puig de Galatzó**, and today the site of an artists' colony. The main road passes the imposing-looking church of Sant Joan Baptista, with its fortified tower. A small side road leads down to the little gravel beach at Port d'Estallencs.

Heading northwards, just outside Banyalbufar is the ★★ **Mirador de Ses Animes** with its 16th-century watchtower (*atalaia*), once part of an effective defence system against pirates and the Barbary corsairs, who raided the islands relentlessly until the beginning of the 19th century. This *mirador* is one of the most popular towers on the Mallorcan coast, and provides a fine view of another artists' colony, **Banyalbufar** (pop. 500). Many of the artists here are from abroad. The town's name is of Moorish origin and means 'small vineyard by the sea', as it was once famed for its white Malvasia wine. Today the terraces are used for fruit and vegetable cultivation. One interesting sight here is the 17th-century **Palau de la Baronía**, containing the hotel of the same name. Next to the hotel entrance, a flight of steps leads down into the peaceful inner courtyard with its battlemented watchtower and well.

The 16th-century watchtower

From Banyalbufar the route veers away from the coast across the Coll de Sa Bastida. Shortly afterwards there is a fine view as far as the **Teix** (1,062m/3,484ft) and the

The terraces of Banyalbufar

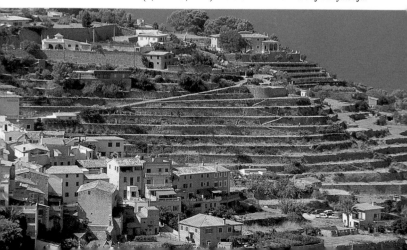

estates of Miramar and Son Marroig. Near Esporles is the old country estate of ★★★ **La Granja** (daily 10am–6pm). The former manor dates from the 17th century and today is one of the island's most popular tourist attractions. The area around La Granja was famed for its water as long ago as Roman times. The Moors, who named the place Alpich, improved the irrigation system and built several water mills.

After the island was taken by James I, La Granja became the property of Count Nuno Sanç, who handed it on to the Cistercian Order shortly afterwards. The monks built Mallorca's first ever monastery here, then in 1447 they moved to Palma and sold the estate to the Vidas, a patrician family. Around 200 years later the property was sold again, this time to the Fortuny family who turned it into a splendid manor house. During the 1960s La Granja was restored for the purposes of tourism.

The peaceful, leafy gardens with their numerous fountains are wonderful to explore, and the manor house itself contains over 40 rooms. The best time to visit is early morning or late afternoon, when the excursion coaches have left. The interior is quite magnificent and gives a good idea of how the Mallorcan landed nobility once must have lived. The rooms and banqueting halls are filled with valuable furniture and paintings. The **house chapel** is also worth a visit, as is the former **torture chamber**. Children might prefer to stay outside and enjoy the donkeys, pigs, wild goats and sheep.

There's a choice of routes back from La Granja: either via the scenic mountain route through Puigpunyent, Galilea and Capdellà, or along the less tiring but also less scenically interesting road that goes to Palma via Esporles and Establiments.

One of the most famous *llogarets* (tiny villages) on the island is ★★ **Galilea**, an enchanting little community 460m (1,509ft) up in the mountains. Almost half the 400 inhabitants are foreigners, who have bought old restored farmhouses or built new villas with swimming pools on the slopes around the centre of the village. The church of the Immaculate Conception dates from 1810. Sunday is a good day to be here, when the restaurants on the village square prepare delicious *tapas* (*see Food and Drink, page 89*) for hungry churchgoers.

The route then continues via the tiny municipality of **Capdellà**, with its elegant villas and luxuriant gardens, back to Peguera.

From La Granja it's possible to connect with Route 3 of this book, either along the C710 coast road to Valldemossa or via Esporles and S'Esglaieta (*see page 34*).

Shades of the past, La Granja

The house chapel

The mountain village of Galilea

Route 3

On the trail of famous visitors

Palma Nova – Valldemossa – Deià – Sóller – (Port de Sóller) – Alfàbia – Bunyola – Palma Nova (approx 90km/55 miles) *See map on page 28*

This is one of the classic routes on Mallorca, and one of the best the island has to offer in terms of both scenery and sights. The first stop is the highlight of the whole trip in the gentle valley of Valldemossa with its famous Carthusian monastery, where George Sand and Frédéric Chopin once stayed. The artists' colony at Deià is much quieter, and the pubs there are frequented by creative people from all over the world. From Deià the route descends into the broad valley of Sóller, with its orange plantations. On the way back to Palma the Serra de Alfàbia must be crossed, unless the planned tunnel has been completed. The winding road across the Coll de Sóller with its many hairpins is a challenging drive. The luxuriant gardens of Alfàbia, or the peaceful little town of Bunyola, offer relaxation after the rigours of the road.

Son Marroig near Deià

33

The route begins at the small holiday resort of **Palma Nova**, with its parks and private villas, which has almost completely merged with the neighbouring resort of Magaluf. Most of the tourists here are English, and there's a huge range of entertainment available, including the Nemo submarine, the BCM Superdisco, and the Marineland and Aquapark water adventure parks.

Coming from the direction of Palma Nova, pass the coastal resorts of Portals Nous, Illetes and Cala Major. It takes

Souvenir plates at Valldemossa

20 minutes to reach the northwest coast of Mallorca by car from Palma's northern suburbs. The Fiora glass factory is just beyond the idyllic village of **S'Esglaieta**. Before Valldemossa there is a broad bend, and the road becomes very steep and straight. The jumble of houses around the Carthusian monastery can already be seen in the distance.

In the monastery cloisters

The ★★★ **Carthusian monastery of Valldemossa**, surrounded by cypresses and a huddle of ochre-coloured houses, lies at the heart of this green valley high in the mountains. People come here from all over the world to see the monastery cells in which George Sand and Frédéric Chopin stayed, wrote and composed. The community was originally a Moorish settlement called Villaverde, and Valldemossa and Deià formed one municipality until well into the 16th century. Many of the palaces and manor houses here date from the 16th and 17th centuries.

The monastery was founded in 1399 by Martí of Aragón, who left the former royal palace (built by James II for his son Sanxo) and the surrounding lands to Carthu-

The library

sian monks. From 1399 to 1767 the monks lived only in this old part, but later added a church, cloister and cells to the new one. After church property was confiscated in 1835, the monastery was dissolved and the monks expelled, then the state sold off different parts of the building to private investors. Each of the cells is still privately owned. Some are museums, others are used as summer residences.

George Sand, whose real name was Baroness Dupin-Dudevant, described Mallorca as 'the most beautiful place I have ever lived'. She set off for the island from Paris in 1838, accompanied by her two children, hoping that a change of climate would help her sickly son, and also

Chopin's manuscripts

her lover Frédéric Chopin who was suffering from tuberculosis. They travelled via Barcelona and Palma. After a brief stay on the outskirts of the island's capital, the unmarried couple then set off for the monastery of Valldemossa, which had been desecularised three years before. During two wet and windy winter months, George Sand wrote down many of her impressions of Mallorca, and her collected notes were later published as *A Winter on Mallorca*.

Chopin composed his famous *Raindrop Prelude* on an old piano from the village because his own Pleyel had been held up by customs and did not arrive until just before his departure. Chopin initially expressed much enthusiasm for his new refuge: 'I am going to be living in a wonderful monastery in one of the most beautiful places on earth,' he wrote to his friends. This positive attitude soon turned to one of despair, though. During the rainy season, which began at the end of December, Chopin's health promptly deteriorated. 'My cell is like a coffin,' he wrote to his publisher in Paris soon afterwards. To make matters worse, the inhabitants of Valldemossa were openly hostile to the unmarried pair, selling them food at inflated prices, and George Sand was forced to take the coach to Palma to go shopping. Nevertheless, despite the cold and damp, George Sand was still effusive about the beauties of the Mallorcan landscape: 'Nature here has fashioned all that a poet or painter could ever have dreamt of.'

Chopin's cell

Meanwhile, the inhabitants of Valldemossa were becoming increasingly wary of Chopin's mysterious illness, and rather resented Sand for strolling through the village wearing men's trousers and smoking cigars. The feeling of hostility was mutual. 'We could have lived on good terms with the local people had we gone to church. That would not have stopped them from taking every opportunity to cheat us, but at least it would have stopped them from throwing stones at our heads from behind bushes whenever we walked by,' noted Sand. The Mallorcans never forgave her for these and many other critical remarks, but their descendants today are making a fortune out of the couple's stay.

35

Allow at least two hours for any visit to the monastery. The tour includes a visit to the monastery church, the former pharmacy, the cells where Chopin and George Sand stayed and the municipal museum. King Sanxo's royal palace has a separate entrance and is a good place for a breather before tackling the monastery proper.

Valldemossa view

Construction work on the **monastery church** began in the middle of the 18th century. The frescoes in its dome are by Bayeu, a brother-in-law of Goya. The statue of the Virgin on the high altar is by Adrià Ferran. One of the most fascinating rooms in the monastery is the 17th-century ★★ **pharmacy** with its finely painted ceiling. The jars, some of which are Catalan ceramic with blue-and-white decoration, others Mallorcan glass, still contain medicines dating from that time. After the expulsion of the monks in 1835, brother Gabriel Oliver kept the pharmacy going to serve the population of Valldemossa and the surrounding villages. Alongside the glass and porcelain, there are also large, painted, wooden trunks originally used to store medicinal herbs.

The pharmacy

Each of the monastery cells consists of three rooms with its own section of garden, although the **abbot's cell** is considerably larger than the others. The cell in which the abbot used to read Holy Mass contains a woodcut of the Madonna and Child, and a plaque on the wall reminds visitors that Jovellanos, the Spanish author and politician, lived here during his exile (1801–2). The monastery **library** next door was where the monks used to assemble. This was one of the few opportunities they had to communicate with each other during their otherwise totally secluded life. Each monk was allowed to keep up to three books in his cell. The walls of the library are decorated with **ceramics** from various regions of Spain.

Ceramics in the library

The highlights here, though, are the 16th-century triptych (Flemish school) and the 15th-century ivory retable showing the marriage of Marie de Montpelier to Pedro of Aragón. The **audience chamber** was where the abbot received officials, bailiffs and administrators from the lands surrounding the monastery. The room contains some fine Mallorcan furniture (eg the abbot's chair), several historic documents and also some valuable paintings including a *Flight from Egypt* by Bassano, *The Martyrdom of St Stephen* by Lucas, and *St Andrew* by Francisco Herrera. On the easel is a painting of St Bruno, the founder of the Carthusian Order. The **foundation stone** for the new building dating from 1717 can be seen in the gardens outside the abbot's cell.

★★ **Cells 2 and 4**, where Frédéric Chopin and George Sand lived and worked, are the most celebrated. The first room contains furniture and religious paintings, a legacy of the Carthusians, and the next room has a fascinating collection of sketches, photographs, original scores, portraits and handwritten letters. Several locks of Chopin's hair (a present to George Sand) and a handmade ivory comb are revered here as tiny works of art. On one side of the room is the Mallorcan piano that Chopin played

Chopin's piano

until his Pleyel piano arrived. The Steinway piano also in this room is used for the Chopin Festival held each year. The garden is full of roses, lilies, cacti and citrus trees, and the view from the terrace extends as far as the plain of Palma. The third room contains a handwritten copy of George Sand's *A Winter in Mallorca*, and also an extensive library with detailed information about the life and work of the two artists. In cell No 4 is Chopin's original Pleyel piano with its certificate of authenticity, and also more manuscripts, books and paintings.

The cells that follow are part of the **municipal museum**. The first room contains the printing press and collection of relief plates belonging to the Guasp printing works, founded in Palma in 1579, and the oldest in Europe. The books, photographs, portraits and manuscripts in the adjacent room document the stay of the Archduke Ludwig Salvator on Mallorca (*see page 38*). The **art gallery** contains several paintings of the Mallorcan landscape by local artists, and the new contemporary art section, with its entrance staircase lined by colourful Miró posters, has an exhibition of works by Max Ernst, Antoni Saura, Hans Hartung, Joan Miró and Henry Moore.

37

Next to the monastery complex is the ★★ **Palau del Rei Sanxo** (daily except Sunday 9.30am–1.20pm and 2.30–5pm, extended in summer), entered via a separate doorway and a small leafy courtyard. The first hall is where 15-minute piano performances of Chopin's works are given hourly during July and August (except Monday and Thursday) by young and usually gifted pianists as part of the Chopin Festival. The Chopin Society is sponsored by UNESCO, and its president is Queen Sofia of Spain.

After the concert the palace can be visited. It was built on the ruins of an old fortress that once belonged to the Moor Muza. King James II had the palace built for his son Sanxo, who suffered from asthma. The Mallorcan royal family later used the building as a base for hunting and falconry expeditions in the Teix Valley. The music hall was renovated in 1870 and decorated with works by the Mallorcan painter Ricard Ankermann (1842–1907). Famous guests at the palace included the Spanish philosophers and poets Azorin, Rusinyol and Unamuno.

Those tempted to take a break from the bustle around the monastery should stroll down to the narrow, cobbled streets in the lower part of the town. Just past the 13th-century church of **Sant Bartomeu**, in the Carrer Rectoria, is a monument to the island's patron saint Catalina Thomàs. She was born in 1531 at house No 5, now a chapel. A farmer's daughter, she was renowned for her humility. A patron took her to Palma, where she worked in

Scenes from the life of Saint Catalina Thomàs

a palace before becoming a nun. She was canonised after her death in 1574. Numerous tiles on the house walls here depict scenes from her life.

One very refreshing detour from Valldemossa is to take the narrow road that leads from the village down to ★ **Port de Valldemossa**, a small gravel bay 6km (3½ miles) away. It provides a good opportunity to wind down and relax with a delicious meal by the beach and a swim in the crystal-clear water of the bay.

Travel north from Valldemossa now above the coast, past the estates of Son Moragues, Miramar and S'Estaca, all of which used to belong to the Austrian Archduke Ludwig Salvator (*see below*), as did ★★ **Son Marroig** (April to September 9.30am–2.30pm and 4.30–8pm, October to March until 6pm, closed Sunday). This 18th-century manor house high above the Na Foradada peninsula is open to visitors, and the museum inside it contains a collection of manuscripts, photographs, drawings and other exhibits documenting the archduke's stay on the island. The ★★ **view** from the house is superb, and in the attractive grounds there is a small Ionic temple of white Carrara marble. The famous Sunset Concerts are held here in Son Marroig from May onwards, and in July and August several classical music concerts are performed as part of the Deià summer festival.

Known familiarly to the locals even today as S'Arxiduc, the Austrian Archduke Ludwig Salvator was one of the world's most famous experts on the Mediterranean. At the end of the 19th century he collated his painstaking research, and his detailed guide to the Balearic archipelago in seven volumes was published in Leipzig in 1897. The two-volume distillation of the work won the archduke a gold medal at the World Fair in Paris and is still the most comprehensive guide to the islands.

Ludwig Salvator of Austria-Tuscany was born in Florence in 1847, the son of Archduke Leopold II of Tuscany and Archduchess Maria Antonieta of Bourbon. One of the earliest dropouts, he turned his back on court life in Vienna and devoted himself to travel and the study of foreign cultures. He lived at his villa near Trieste, at Brandeis Castle on the Elbe in Bohemia, on his steam-driven yacht *Nixe* and also on Mallorca. His scientific exploration trips took him around the world, and he was not only a mariner, geographer, landowner, writer and artist but also a great lover of nature and one of the earliest ecologists. He arrived on Mallorca for the first time in 1867 and was captivated by it. He came again in 1871 and in the following year purchased his first house, Miramar. This was followed by the acquisition of two more estates at S'Estaca and Son

Marroig, until he finally owned more than 11km (6 miles) of Mallorca's northwest coast. The Na Foradada peninsula below Son Marroig also formed part of his estate.

Enchanted by the natural beauties of the island, the archduke often bought large tracts of land to save trees from being chopped down. He not only studied the local mores and traditions but also liked to wear simple peasant dress himself in order to facilitate communication with the local people. The archduke was just as enchanted by Catalina Hómar, the daughter of a Valldemossa carpenter, so much so that he bought her the estate at S'Estaca. Today the building belongs to actor Michael Douglas. There is a fine walk originally laid out by Ludwig Salvator, which begins at Valldemossa and crosses the Serra de Tramuntana. Many streets and squares of the island still bear the name of its famous adoptive son, and 1994 was the 'Year of the Archduke', with a large exhibition in La Llotja in Palma devoted to his life and work.

Deià church

39

On the slopes of the 1,062-m (3,484-ft) high mountain massif of the Teix stands ★★★ **Deià** (pop. 600), one of the most picturesque villages in Mallorca. At the centre of the village is the small rise with a church on top surrounded by ochre-coloured houses that is so typical of Mallorca. The little main street, lined with cafés, restaurants and galleries, skirts the base of it. Narrow, winding streets lead to what is perhaps the finest ★★ **cemetery** on the island.

The cemetery in bloom

Deià's church of Sant Joan Baptista received its present appearance in the 18th century, and inside there is a *St Sebastian* by Adrià Ferran. There used to be a Moorish settlement in the Deià area before the island was conquered by James I. The Cistercians based themselves here during the Middle Ages, and later the Visconti family from Italy (mentioned by Dante in his *Divina Comedia*) chose Deià as their place of residence. In 1583 the municipality became independent of neighbouring Valldemossa. Various towers and fortified structures stand as reminders of the pirate raids during the 17th century.

Since the end of the 18th century Deià has gradually developed into an internationally famed artists' colony. The Archduke Ludwig Salvator was followed by the Catalan writer and painter Santiago Rusinyol, the writer Anaïs Nin and the American painter and archaeologist William Waldren. The most famous of its residents, however, was the poet and novelist Robert Graves (1895– 1985), who came to Deià in 1929 when the success of his World War I autobiography *Goodbye to All That* enabled him to make Mallorca his permanent home. His sad love poems are ranked alongside those of WB Yeats as the finest produced in the English language in the 20th century. In the 1960s, he and William Waldren founded a **museum of art and**

The tomb of Robert Graves

Stony comfort at Cala Deià

Llucalcari: tile detail and houses

Freshly squeezed juices

archaeology at Deià, with exhibitions of works by the Deu des Teix artists' group and archaeological finds from the Sa Muleta cavern. Robert Graves died in 1985, and is buried in the small cemetery in Deià. His tombstone bears the simple inscription 'Poeta'.

The young artists here exhibit their work in the small galleries in the village or in the Residencia, Deià's luxury hotel (*see page 102*). Those wishing to mingle with the young and gifted should visit Christian's Bar, Café Sa Fonda or the Bar Las Palmeras. In July and August, during the Deià music festival, international stars give performances in the small church on the hillside.

The narrow road that leads down to the tiny gravel beach of **Cala Deià** is recommended only to drivers with a head for heights. The beach is popular with people from the village, who sit around on the uncomfortable rocks or enjoy fresh cuttlefish on the terrace of the nearby restaurant.

★★ **Llucalcari**, once described by the Archduke Ludwig Salvator as 'one of the finest little corners of the world', makes another good detour. It is a tiny village with a handful of stone houses, several massive square towers once used as defences against corsairs, and the little church of Mare de Déu dels Desemperats.

The C710 curves its way over the **Coll de Galera** now, before leading downhill into the valley of Sóller. This was once considered one of the most attractive roads on the entire island, but the stretch has recently been widened. At the end of this section of road the C711 leads off to the left in the direction of Port de Sóller. Carry straight on at this point, though, and very soon the town of **Sóller** (pop. 10,000) comes into view.

The Moorish name for Sóller was Suliar (sea-shell). It lies in a valley basin between the 1,445-m (4,740-ft) high **Puig Major**, the highest mountain on the island, and the round bay of Port de Sóller. Before the tourists discovered this town, the inhabitants were earning a great deal from cultivating citrus fruit. The main export market was the South of France, and freshly squeezed juices can still be enjoyed today by visitors to Sóller's busy Plaça de la Constitució. The high facades of the Banco Central Hispano and the church of Sant Bartomeu (16th-century) dominate this square, which is lined with cafés, bakeries and newsagents. The ★ **Orange Express**, Sóller's vintage tram, rattles its way across the centre of the square, connecting the town with the harbour 5km (3 miles) away.

The town's ethnological museum, the **Museu de Sóller** (Monday to Friday 4–6pm, Saturday morning, closed Sunday), occupies a manor house built in 1740 (Carrer

de la Mar 13). In 1992 the natural science museum and the botanical gardens (Museu Balear de Ciències Naturales i Jardí Botànic de Sóller) were opened along the C711 ring road around the town. The gardens have an interesting collection of aromatic herbs, and plants from various different regions of the Balearic archipelago (Tuesday to Saturday 10.30am–1.30pm and 5–8pm, Sunday 10.30am–1.30pm). Sóller's war memorial at the junction between Port de Sóller and Port de Pollença is a reminder of the brave women of the town who fought at their husband's sides in 1571 to stop an invasion by 1,700 Turkish pirates. This act of heroism is celebrated on 10 May each year in the 'Christians and Moors' (*Cristians i Morus*) festival, when the people of Sóller re-enact the battle and drive the Moorish pirates out of the town.

In the Gardens of Alfàbia

41

A narrow-gauge railway links Sóller to Palma, with trains leaving at least five times a day. The journey lasts an hour.

Sóller railway station and a restful journey to Palma

From Sóller the road winds its way up to the 496-m (1,627-ft) high Coll de Sóller. The Bar S'Hostalet at the top of the pass is a good place to stop and enjoy a superb view of the plain of Palma. At the end of the hairpins at the foot of the pass, where the new tunnel has been driven through the rock, are the marvellously peaceful ★★ Gardens of Alfàbia (November to March 9.30am–5pm, April to October 9.30am–6.30pm, closed Sunday), which date back to Moorish times. The Moorish vizirs often used to stroll through these beautiful gardens, and they also devised a very clever system of irrigation. There are palm trees, shady cypresses and Aleppo pine trees, as well as several species of ornamental plant.

Although the park has been somewhat neglected in recent years, it still retains its special charm and tranquillity. An avenue of plane trees leads from the car park to the

Along the leafy avenue

manor house with its large baroque facade. The gardens are entered via a palm-lined flight of steps, and soon all that can be heard is birdsong and the sound of water splashing in the fountains. The route through the gardens continues via a leafy avenue to an area with flowerbeds, bushes and a goldfish pond. Lemon and olive trees grow on the terraces surrounding the gardens, with Aleppo pine trees growing on the slopes higher up.

The rooms of the 15th-century manor house can be visited, including the library, with its ancient books on history, art, literature and the theatre. One of the most treasured possessions is a 14th-century Gothic ★ **chair** carved in oak. On the back, there is a tree with owls resting in its branches, and beneath it a prince is depicted playing chess with a woman.

After the island was captured by the Christians from the Moors, Alfàbia belonged to the Caballeros de Santa Cilias, who supported James III. This noble family was succeeded by the Zafortezas, whose portraits are seen hanging in the banqueting hall, with its colourful roof-beams. The ceiling of the entrance portal has Arabic panelling from the Almohad epoch (1170) with ivory inlay.

A popular apéritif

Shady square in Bunyola

The route continues to ★★ **Bunyola**, originally famed not only for its wine (the name Bunyola comes from the Latin for 'little vineyard') but also for its olive oil. At the end of the 19th century Bunyola produced 36 percent of Mallorca's olive oil. There are also several almond and carob plantations. The distillery, founded by Antonio Nadal in 1898, produces Mallorca's famous herbal liqueurs and the popular apéritif, **Palo Tunel**. The logo – a train coming out of a tunnel – can be seen at the entrance to the old factory building. Sa Plaça, the town's main square, is a good place to follow the example of the locals and while away the time under the shady plane trees. The church on the square has a valuable 15th-century alabaster statue of the Virgin on its high altar. Directly opposite, two palm trees flank the attractive town hall, and next door is a house with a fine wrought-iron balcony.

At the end of May and beginning of June Bunyola celebrates its traditional May festival, with dancing and theatrical events. The fiesta in honour of St Matthew, the town's patron saint, takes place at the end of September and heralds the start of the classical-music festival that lasts into November.

A worthwhile detour from Bunyola is to take a small side-road on to the P210 into the apple orchards of the valley of Orient. The little mountain village of Orient is 10km (6 miles) away from Bunyola, and has a small hotel and several good restaurants (*see page 60*).

Route 4

The wild Serra de Tramuntana

Port de Sóller – Fornalutx – Sa Calobra – Monestir de Lluc – Pollença – Cap de Formentor – Alcúdia (approx 110km/ 68 miles) *See map on pages 44–5*

This route leads through the grandiose mountain scenery of the Serra de Tramuntana. Just a few kilometres out of Port de Sóller it passes the picturesque village of Fornalutx and the Ses Barques observation point. Then the road starts to wind uphill, and pine forests gradually give way to rough landscape high in the mountains, with towering peaks and sparkling reservoirs. Driving along this road needs a lot of concentration – it's considered one of the most dangerous on the island – and a particularly sharp hairpin marks the start of the descent into the narrow Sa Calobra ravine. In the Monestir de Lluc, the spiritual heart of the island, the monks look after the mind, body and soul of their many visitors and pilgrims. The mountain road then leads gently down to the historic little town of Pollença with its intact Roman bridge, interesting art galleries and many fine restaurants.

From the Port de Pollença the route then continues as far as Mallorca's northernmost point, the Cap de Formentor, distinguished by its bizarre rock formations. The bay of Cala de Sant Vicenç is also near Pollença, as are the Puig de Santa Maria and the old ruined fortress of Castell del Rei. The coast road along the broad Badia de Pollença leads to neighbouring Alcúdia, which the Romans used to call Pollentia. Its old town centre is enclosed by massive medieval walls, and outside the gates are the ruins of a Roman settlement. An attractive detour from

Festival time in Fornalutx

The Orange Express at Port de Sóller

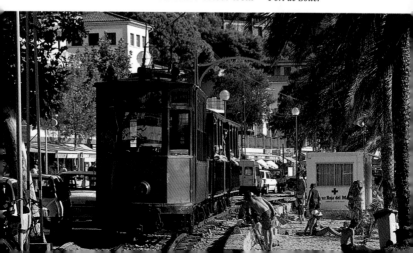

Sangria at Port de Sóller

44

Aspects of Fornalutx

The bay at Sa Calobra

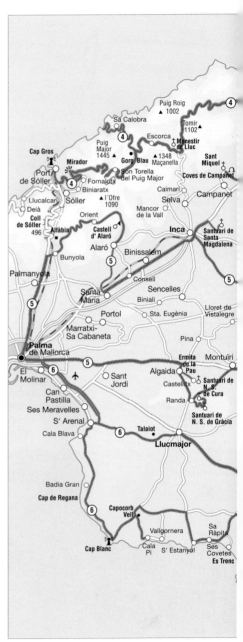

Puig Roig
▲ 1002
Sa Calobra
④
Tomir ▲
1102
Escorca
Monestir
de Lluc
Cap Gros
Puig
Major
1445 ▲
Gorg Blau
▲ 1348
Maçanella
Sant
Miquel
Mirador
Son Torella
del Puig Major
Coves de Campanet
Port
de Sóller
④
Fornalutx
Biniaratx
Caimari
Campanet
Llucalcari
Sóller
▲ l'Ofre
1090
Selva
Deià
Mancor
de la Vall
Inca
Santuari de
Santa
Magdalena
Orient
Coll
de Sóller
496
Alfàbia
Castell
d'Alaró
Alaró
Binissalem
Bunyola
⑤
Palmanyola
Consell
⑤
Santa
Maria
Sencelles
Biniali
Lloret de
Vistalegre
Portol
Sta. Eugènia
Marratxi-
Sa Cabaneta
Pina
Palma
de Mallorca
⑤
Ermita
de la
Pau
Montuïri
El
Molinar
⑥
Sant
Jordi
Algaida
Castellitx
Santuari de
N. S.
de Cura
Can
Pastilla
Ses Meravelles
Randa
S'Arenal
Santuari de
N. S. de Gràcia
Cala Blava
⑥
Talaiot
Llucmajor
Badia Gran
Cap de Regana
⑥
Capocorb
Vell
Vallgornera
Sa
Ràpita
Cala
Pi
Ses
Covetes
Cap Blanc
S'Estanyol
Es Trenc

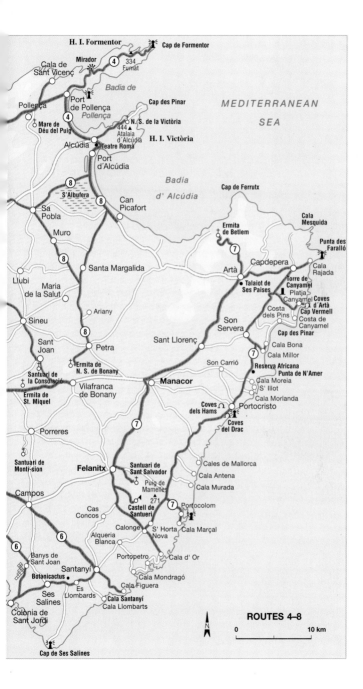

H. I. Formentor

Cap de Formentor

Mirador

4 334 Fumat

Cala de Sant Vicenç

Badia de

MEDITERRANEAN

Cap des Pinar

Pollença

Port de Pollença
Pollença

SEA

4

N. S. de la Victòria

Mare de Déu del Puig

444 Atalaia d'Alcúdia

H. I. Victòria

Alcúdia

Teatre Romà

Port d'Alcúdia

8

Badia
d' Alcúdia

Cap de Ferrutx

S'Albufera

8

Can Picafort

Sa Pobla

Ermita de Betlem

Cala Mesquida

Muro

7

Punta des Faralló

8

Santa Margalida

Artà

Capdepera

Cala Rajada

Llubi

Maria de la Salut

Talaiot de Ses Païses

Torre de Canyamel

Ariany

Platja Canyamel

Coves d'Artà

Sineu

8

Son Servera

Costa dels Pins

Cap Vermell
Costa de Canyamel

Sant Joan

Petra

Sant Llorenç

7

Cap des Pinar

Santuari de la Consolació

Ermita de N. S. de Bonany

Son Carrió

Cala Bona
Cala Millor

Ermita de St. Miquel

Vilafranca de Bonany

Manacor

Reserva Africana
Punta de N'Amer
Cala Moreia
S' Illot
Cala Morlanda

Porreres

7

Coves dels Hams

Portocristo

Coves del Drac

Santuari de Monti-sion

Felanitx

Santuari de Sant Salvador

Cales de Mallorca

Campos

Puig de Mamelles

271

Cala Antena

Cala Murada

Cas Concos

Castell de Santueri

7

Portocolom

6

Calonge

S' Horta Nova

Cala Marçal

6

Alqueria Blanca

Banys de Sant Joan

Portopetro

Cala d' Or

Botanicactus

Santanyí

Ses Salines

Es Llombards

Cala Mondragó
Cala Figuera

Colònia de Sant Jordi

Cala Santanyí
Cala Llombarts

N

ROUTES 4–8

0   10 km

Cap de Ses Salines

Cap Gros lighthouse

Tying up at Port de Sóller

Fornalutx coat of arms

Alcúdia is Cap des Pinar, with its Ermita de la Victòria. The route then ends at Port d'Alcúdia, where there is an old harbour and also the longest and finest sandy beach in the Mediterranean.

The circular bay of ★ **Port de Sóller** is the only protected harbour along the jagged northwest coast of the island. Down at the quayside the fishermen can be observed mending their blue nets, and the excursion boats travel from here to the nearby pebble bays of Cala Tuent and Sa Calobra. The white lighthouse at Cape Gros guards the entrance to the bay. The sandy beach at Port de Sóller is not one of the best on the island, but the harbour has successfully retained the atmosphere of an old-fashioned resort. The changing cabins on the beach are just as antiquated as the charming paintings hung in the bars to extol the virtues of their food and drink.

The C710 begins at the war memorial at the Sóller/Port de Sóller/Port de Pollença junction, and from here the route leads up to some of the highest mountain passes in the Serra de Tramuntana. The turn-off to the mountain village of Fornalutx comes after 6km (3½ miles). Cars can be parked either at the entrance to the village, outside the Can Antuna restaurant, or in the car park next to the square fortification tower. The sleepy village of ★★ **Fornalutx**, on the southern side of the 1,445-m (4,740-ft) high Puig Major, lies in the middle of fragrant orange groves. Fornalutx is considered the prettiest village in Spain and is a national monument. The idyllic stone houses have a high price tag on them, and new buildings or even alterations to existing structures are subject to strict regulations. Roughly one third of the 600 inhabitants are foreigners, many of them English and German.

The locals meet up at the Bar Deportivo on the Plaça Espanya. The vaulted cellar directly opposite was formerly a prison. The square is dominated by the church of Santa Maria, completed in 1639 and the small grocery shop sells instructive brochures about the history of this delightful little village. Walk down through its narrow streets to the Carrer des Vicari Solivellas where the wash-house and also the old town hall can be seen. A small flight of steps outside the Casal de Munt, at Carrer del Metge Mayol 10, was originally built to help riders mount their horses and mules. The projecting roofs at Carrer Sa Font No 7 are decorated with old painted tiles. Unfortunately the 17th-century red clay drawings have faded, but various motifs can still be made out.

The village is surrounded by orange and olive groves stretching away as far as the eye can see. The land around this tiny village was terraced by the Moors, and narrow

The beach at Torrent de Pareis

hiking paths lead to the neighbouring communities of Binibassí and Biniaraitx, both of them of Moorish origin and both almost as pretty as Fornalutx itself.

The observation point known as ★★ **Mirador de Ses Barques** was created in 1961, and the view it affords of the valley, town and harbour in Sóller as far as the old watchtower by the sea is breathtaking. Just sit back on the restaurant terrace here and revel in the landscape. There is also a very good hiking route that leads from the *mirador* down to Cala Tuent, by the sea.

47

The road now goes through a series of curves as it climbs the slopes of the **Puig Major** (1,445m/4,740ft), Mallorca's highest mountain. A tunnel cuts through the Serra de Torellas, passing some buildings belonging to the Spanish air force and also the road leading to the summit itself (a military area, closed to traffic).

The two reservoirs of Gorg Blau and Cúber – both vital to the island's water supply – sparkle against the rough mountain landscape. They are connected to each other by a canal. After Gorg Blau the road enters another tunnel and soon afterwards reaches the turn-off to Sa Calobra. The ★★ **road to Sa Calobra** now winds its way along a distance of 11km (9 miles), from the highest peaks of the Serra down to the bay of Sa Calobra and the ★★ **Torrent de Pareis**, a wild-water ravine surrounded by cliffs which ends at a small pebble beach. The difference in altitude along this stretch is a full 800m (2,624ft), and the route encompasses an extremely notorious hairpin on the way with a 300° curve.

Hairpin bends to Sa Calobra

Torrent de Pareis ravine

Later the Caval Bernat appears, a narrow defile flanked by two gigantic pieces of rock through which hundreds of rental cars and buses pass daily. The handful of houses at Sa Calobra, grouped around the little bay at the end of the road, are barely able to cope with the steady stream of visitors. Nearby Cala Tuent is much more tranquil. Halfway between the two tiny villages is the 13th-century Romanesque church of Sant Llorenç. A word of warning: the road to Sa Calobra is one of the island's biggest tourist attractions, and should be avoided between 10am and 3pm during the high season because of the sheer volume of traffic.

Return from Sa Calobra to the C710, and drive past Escorça, the smallest village in Mallorca (pop. 200), before taking the turn-off to the ★★ **Monestir de Lluc**. The 17th-century monastery church contains a statuette called La Moreneta, similar to the one at Montserrat near Barcelona. According to legend, it was discovered by an Arab boy named Lluc whose family had been converted to Christianity after James I invaded in the 13th century. The boy brought the statuette to the Romanesque church of Sant Pere in Escorça, but it kept returning miraculously to the place where he had originally found it.

Monestir de Lluc

The monastery was built on the site under James I, and today it is the most important place of pilgrimage on Mallorca. Visitors stream to Lluc to visit the Madonna from every corner of the island, especially on Sundays. They also listen to performances by the Blavets, Lluc's famous boys' choir, and dine at the restaurant here. The monastery has more than 100 cells, which are all available as overnight accommodation. The monastery museum contains several archaeological finds dating from the Talayotic period, and also several Roman and Punic exhibits, including ceramics and coins. Another room contains a small natural science collection.

Local entertainment

The road, well-surfaced now, goes uphill along a series of curves through oak forests and then descends gently towards the Vall de Son March, and the town of ★ **Pollença**. The intact Roman bridge outside the town centre is a reminder of Pollença's Roman past. Sunday is the most pleasant day of the week here, as after Mass in the church on the Plaça Major, the locals can buy fresh fruit and vegetables in the marketplace. They then carry their heavy shopping baskets off to the Café Espanyol (Plaça Major 2) for a delicious breakfast. Narrow streets lead from the square to the tiny Plazuela de la Almuina, with its cockerel fountain. The bird is the symbol of the town, and can be seen on all the coats of arms. The 365 steps leading from Pollença's town hall up to the Calvary are lined by slim cypresses, and those strong enough to make it to the top will be rewarded by a stunning panoramic view.

Calvary steps in Pollença

The **municipal museum** (Tuesday to Sunday 11am–1pm, July to September 11am–1pm and 5.20–8.30pm, closed Sunday afternoon) is housed inside an old Do-minican monastery, and its exhibits include a collection of paintings, sculpture and an interesting carpet made of sand – a present from the Dalai Lama. The archaeological section is just as interesting as it contains finds from the prehistoric site at Son Maimó as well as curious wood sculptures shaped like bulls, which were probably used as sarcophagi around 3,500 years ago.

Pollença church

The **church**, with its barrel vault, was completed in 1620. Its organ dates from the 17th century and the sacristy contains Gothic painted panels, Romanesque sculpture and 16th-century embroidery. The monastery cloister is the venue for the town's annual classical music festival, begun in 1961 by the violinist Philip Newman. The excellent acoustics combined with the unique atmosphere of the cloister make concerts here a memorable experience (concerts held between August and mid-September).

Outside the monastery complex are the gardens of Joan March Severa, with their square tower and fascinating collection of Balearic plants. Pollença has several art galleries worth visiting, and also many good restaurants.

49

An interesting detour from Pollença is the 333-m (1,092-ft) high ★★ **Puig de Santa Maria**, with its ruined convent, the Santuari del Puig. The path up to the convent begins 2km (1¼ miles) out of town, and it takes a good hour to reach the top. The first 3km (2 miles) can be travelled by car if preferred. The walls along the last section of the route are a good introduction to the skills of Mallorca's *margers* (wall-builders, *see page 84*). Visitors who tackle the steep ascent are rewarded by a superb ★★ **view**, stretching as far as the Serra de Tramuntana, Cap de Formentor, the plain of Sa Pobla and the two bays of Alcúdia and Pollença. Several parts of the convent complex remain, including some fortified walls, a tower, the Gothic refectory and the Gothic chapel with its statue of the Virgin. The remains of an old mill can also be seen. In 1348 several pious women settled on top of this mountain, and the convent was built here in 1371 under the supervision of abbess Floreta Ricomana. The path leading to the top was laid out in 1391.

View from Puig de Santa Maria

The convent was highly respected, and soon became one of the foremost sacred buildings on the island. Neither the threat of pirate attack in the 16th century nor a command from the bishop of Palma to move to the island's capital for their own safety succeeded in persuading the pious ladies to leave their holy mountain. The convent was briefly abandoned in 1564, but the nuns soon returned. Accommodation is still available for pilgrims and hikers. There are self catering facilities, a bar and a restaurant (give prior notice of arrival, tel: 971 184132).

Cooling off at Port de Pollença

The **Castell del Rei** (13th–14th centuries), perched on its rock 490m (1,607ft) above sea level to the north of Pollença, is no longer accessible to the public. This fortress, once the last refuge of the kings of Mallorca, is now private property.

The PM220 leads from Pollença in the direction of its harbour, Port de Pollença. Barely 3km (2 miles) outside Pollença a country road branches off to the left in the direction of **Cala de Sant Vicenç**, a holiday resort well worth a visit. Many hotels have been built around the small sandy beaches at Cala Barques, Cala Clara and Cala Carbó in recent years, and the whole area is now known collectively as Cala de Sant Vicenç. Offshore there are several large, rough-looking rocks, and the water has an attractive turquoise shimmer to it. There is an enjoyable walking route from here to the Punta de les Coves Blanques (30 minutes away).

Two sea dogs

Pollença's harbour, **Port de Pollença**, with its old-fashioned villas and stylish hotels, now comes into view. It is a resort with ambitions, but has still succeeded in remaining relatively peaceful. On the Passeig Voramar, with its old one-storeyed summer houses and wooden jetties where the branches of the pine trees almost reach the water, there is a memorial bust of the Catalan painter Hermen Anglada Camarassa, who lived and worked in Pollença for many years. There used to be a small museum devoted to his work in his former home here, but the collection has now been transferred to the arts centre in the Gran Hotel in Palma (*see page 24*).

Port de Pollença marina

An extremely rewarding detour can be made from Pollença to the ★★ **Cap de Formentor**, a peninsula full of bizarre rock formations that juts out to form Mallorca's northernmost point, with steep cliffs on one side and gentle, sandy beaches on the other. The lighthouse at the end of the Cap de Formentor is 20km (12 miles) away from Port de Pollença. The PM221 passes a military area before starting to wind its way up into the rough mountain landscape. After about 5km (3 miles), the ★★ **Mirador des Colomer** appears, an observation point 232m (761ft) above the sea with a marvellous view of the rocky island of Colomer and the weird rock formations along this stretch of the coast. The various observation platforms with their telescopes are connected by flights of steps. The stone plaque on the platform furthest from the road provides geographical information.

Mirador des Colomer

Up on the rocky ridge to the right is the ★ **Atalaia de Albercutx**, another superb observation point. Carry on from the Mirador des Colomer towards Cap de Formentor for about 1½km (1 mile) and then turn right down a narrow, asphalt track; it leads up to the old watchtower, and to one of the finest views on the island.

Back on the main road, roughly 9km (5½ miles) further on, there is a right turn to the Hotel Formentor (*see below*). From this junction it's another 11km (6 miles) to the point itself. The road bears round to the left and then leads through an oak and pine forest, and just before entering the tunnel that leads through the 334-m (1,095-ft) high Fumat mountain there's a good view of the crystal-clear waters of Cala Figuera far below, one of the most unspoilt and inaccessible beaches on the island (*see page 63*). There are lots more places along the route to stop the car and enjoy the view. The lighthouse stands at Mallorca's northernmost point from where Menorca can be seen in clear weather.

On the way back, the ★ **Hotel Formentor** is a good place to stop for a coffee, and its Cala Pi beach is ideal for swimming. This legendary hotel was built in 1928 by the Argentinian architect Adam Diehl. One of the earliest guests was Winston Churchill, who spent the night in a Mallorcan four-poster bed. Many famous people have stayed here since then, including Grace Kelly and the former German chancellor, Helmut Schmidt.

Fishing for fun

Back at the Port de Pollença, follow the pretty coast road around the Bay of Pollença as far as ★★ **Alcúdia**. Known to the Romans as Pollentia, it was renamed Al-Kudia (town on the hill) by the Moors, and its mighty medieval walls, built to withstand pirate attacks, are definitely worth seeing. Enter the town centre through either the Porta de Sant Sebastià or the Porta de Xara. Within the walls and around the Casa Consistorial (town hall) there are several fine 16th- and 17th-century palazzi. The palace known as Can Torró (Carrer d'en Serra 15) has housed an ultra-modern

Pretty Alcúdia

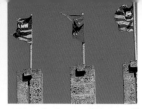

Flying the flags on the town wall

library since 1990. On Sundays there is a good market here, which takes place close to the town walls and along the Passeig de la Mare de Deu de la Victòria, and several of the shops nearby open their doors too.

Next to the town wall is the **church of Sant Jaume**. The rose window on the main facade was once the only source of light (the panes of glass used to be transparent). The stained glass was only added later on, along with the side windows. The church was renovated in 1893. It has an interesting museum, with various Gothic retables (14th- and 15th-century), monstrances, liturgical instruments and several fine examples of wood carving (Tuesday to Sunday 10am–noon).

Beyond the church is the **Roman Museum**. The extensive collection of Roman finds here includes ceramics, glassware, busts, jewellery, coins, cult artefacts, tools and surgical instruments (Museu Monogràfic de Pollentia, Carrer Sant Jaume 30, Tuesday to Friday 10am–1.30pm and 3.30–5.30pm, in summer 5–7pm, Saturday and Sunday 10.30am–1pm).

Roman theatre remains

The ★★ **Roman theatre** (Teatre Roma) is on the road between Alcúdia and Port d'Alcúdia (follow the signposts, then it's a five-minute walk). It was excavated in 1952 by members of the William Bryant Foundation, and the rear facade, the semicircular stage and one of the semicircular viewing stands can still be seen. Pollentia remained under Roman control until the death of Emperor Honorio in AD428, and its decline only began with the arrival of the Vandals, who by 476 had Africa, the Balearic Islands, Sardinia and Sicily under their control. Some more ruins of the old Roman settlement can still be seen on the other side of the by-pass not far from the church. This site was also excavated in 1952 by the American archaeologist William Bryant.

An idyllic side road with some fine views of the Bay of Pollença and Cap Formentor leads northeast from Alcúdia out to the **Cap des Pinar**, with its church of Nostra Senyora de la Victòria, founded in around 1300. From the car park (and restaurant) a path leads up to the ancient Atalaia d'Alcúdia (watchtower) standing in the middle of the peninsula, and to the rock at the tip of the point known as Penya Rotja.

Popular Port d'Alcúdia

Port d'Alcúdia marks the end of this route. Down at the old harbour, it is still just about possible to sense something of the original atmosphere of this erstwhile fishing village, but the rest of the beautiful bay here has fallen prey to tourism, and the broad main road is lined for miles by hotels, souvenir shops, fast-food restaurants, amusement arcades and discotheques.

Route 5

The rural heart of the island

Palma – Algaida – Randa – Montuïri – Vilafranca de Bonany – Sineu – Inca – Binissalem – Santa Maria del Camí – Alaró – Orient – Palma (94km/58 miles) *See map on pages 44–5*

Sineu Art Centre

53

This route leads across the cornfields and pasturelands of Mallorca's fertile central plain, passing through sleepy little villages and busy market towns. Just beyond Palma is the area of the island known as the Pla de Mallorca, with its many windmills. Algaida and Montuïri, tranquil villages situated on hills next to the main road, are both well worth a visit. The first highlight of the route, though, is the visit to the idyllic village of Randa, at the foot of the 543-m (1,78-1ft) high Puig de Randa, also known as the 'mountain of the three hermitages'. Vilafranca de Bonany is the best place to buy fruit and fresh vegetables, and the traditional weekly market at Sineu is also very good. Inca is a busy town with many leather factories and also several excellent *cellers*. On the way back to Palma, the route passes through Binissalem and the little village of Santa Maria del Camí, with its fine cloister in the former monastery of Minimos. From Santa Maria it's possible to take the motorway straight back to Palma, but a return journey via Alaró and Orient is more rewarding.

Watching the world go by in Inca

Leave Palma on the busy road to Manacor, passing the suburb of Son Ferriol, the tiny hamlets of Casa Blanca and Can Fideu and also the **Prehistoric Parc Son Gual**, with its 20 life-sized dinosaurs. Some 19km (11 miles) further on, it's worth stopping at the Vidrerías Gordiola glass factory on the left. Glass-making is an ancient art on

Making Gordiola glass

Millstones from Molí d'en Xina

Monastery at Randa

Mallorca, dating back to the 4th century BC. At the ★ **Gordiola glass factory** visitors can watch glass being melted and blown and see several antique masterpieces of the art in the museum. Many of the products on display in the salerooms are based on these.

The town of **Algaida**, up on a hill on the right-hand side of the main road, has a population of around 3,200. The name is of Moorish origin and means 'forest', an allusion to the thick woods that originally covered the area. At the centre of the town is the imposing 15th-century church of **Sant Pere i Sant Pau**. Its Gothic portal with the rose window and statue of the Virgin is very fine, and there are some weird-looking gargoyles on the side facing the Carrer del Rei. On the outskirts of town is an old mill, Molí d'en Xina, with red roof and wooden sails; it dates from 1738 and has been the headquarters of a young artists' association since 1980. The rooms on the ground floor contain workshops and exhibition rooms, and there is also a video studio. Concerts, lectures, poetry readings and films are regular events (Associació Cultural Algaida, Molí d'en Xina, Carrer de la Ribera 35). Algaida is also a popular destination for Mallorcans at the weekend because of the delicious local food served in its restaurants, many of them former coaching inns.

Before heading back to the main road, a detour should definitely be made at this point to the nearby ★★ **Ermita de la Pau**, and to the monastery mountain of Randa. Shortly after leaving Algaida, follow a small side road up through some shady forest to the hamlet of Castellitx. The road is badly surfaced, but the views are superb. At the top of the hill on the right is the small hermitage of La Pau. The Romanesque chapel was completed in 1243 and is one of the oldest on Mallorca. The inhabitants of Algaida have an annual spring procession to the shrine here.

The route continues along a narrow but well-surfaced road before rejoining the main Algaida–Llucmajor road. Turn left a little further on to go to **Randa** (pop. 250), a small village with a church, a handful of stone houses and several good restaurants. It is situated on the flanks of the 543-m (1,781-ft) high ★ **Puig de Randa**. This mountain, surrounded by cornfields, almond plantations, carob and fig trees, is not only a geographical peculiarity in the otherwise flat southern part of the island, but also an important place of pilgrimage, with its three hermitages, and a fascinating cultural site.

The winding road up the mountain starts behind the Es Recó restaurant in the village. The first building that comes into view is the ★★ **Oratori de Nostra Senyora**

de Gràcia, built towards the end of the 15th century. Inside this pretty white church is an attractively tiled side chapel, with a statue of Santa Anna, and to the right of it a figure representing Sant Antoni Abat, patron saint of pets. The niches at the sides contain some fine painted panels, and high above the main altar the Virgen de Gràcia is seen seated in a shell-shaped niche.

From the terrace of the hermitage there is a splendid view of the flat southeastern part of Mallorca, and sometimes of the island of Cabrera too, though it is usually hidden in the haze. The grounds and the gardens are looked after by a local farmer.

The next stop along the way up the mountain is the hermitage of ★**Sant Honorat**, founded in 1394 by Arnau Desbrull, a nobleman from Inca. Inside the church entrance on the left is the **Sant Crist dels Ermitants**, a carved figure dating from the 14th century which is particularly revered by the Mallorcans. Legend has it that the founder of the hermitage carried it up here in person.

The view from the top

55

At the very top of the mountain is the hermitage of ★★ **Nostra Senyora de Cura**, certainly the most famous of the three. Visit the Sala de Gramàtica. This famous centre of learning was founded at the beginning of the 16th century on the site where the Catalan mystic Ramón Llull had lived as a hermit. Hundreds of students used to learn Latin here, and the vaulted ceiling of the hall dates from that time. The stone floor was renovated in 1935 using stone from the mountain. Exhibits on display in the hermitage include religious paintings, liturgical instruments, ancient books and manuscripts. The ethnological section displays kitchenware and agricultural implements. Next to the Sala de Gramàtica is the chapel, which contains a 17th-century wooden statue of Christ.

Ramón Llull

The hermitage also has a bar and restaurant attached, with a large dining hall and a terrace. The garden contains a selection of old agricultural implements, coaches and wagon wheels as well as a statue of St Francis of Assisi. Four Franciscan monks look after the estate and the visitors. The monastery provides comfortable overnight accommodation, with rooms sleeping 2 to 6 people, at moderate prices.

From Randa it is possible to reach the small town of Montuïri without having to go back via Algaida. **Montuïri** (pop. 2,000) lies on the left-hand side of the C715, and was first mentioned as long ago as the 13th century. The town lived exclusively off agriculture until a few years ago. Today a large number of the inhabitants have administrative jobs or work in the service sector in Palma.

The seven slender mill towers are the symbol of the town. At its centre is the 17th-century church of ★★ **Santa**

Maria. The interior is magnificent, and includes a 16th-century retable by the Valencian painter Mateu Llopis. The Ball de Cossiers is held every August here as part of the fiesta in honour of the town's patron saint, Sant Bartomeu. It is an ancient custom of uncertain origin, and involves six men in historical costume, one of them playing the part of a lady. She is the one who beats the devil in the end.

It is worth making a detour to the ★★ **hermitage of Montesió** above the village of **Porreres**, 7km (4¼ miles) to the south of Montuïri. The distance up the mountain isn't that far (4km/2½ miles), and cars can be parked on the palm-lined terrace outside the hermitage itself. The road was built by the people of Porreres in 1954, and a memorial in the courtyard stands as a reminder to this piece of community work. The single-aisled church contains a white marble statue with a gold crown, the Verge de Montesio, which dates from the 15th century and is much revered. She is the patron saint of Porreres. The courtyard with its attractive fountain gets quite busy at weekends, but otherwise the place is almost deserted. The main square in Porreres, with its cafés, town hall and church, is very lively in contrast.

Ready for picking

Backtrack now briefly to the C715, past greenhouses, fruit plantations and vineyards and 1km (½ mile) along the main road, there is a turn-off on the left signposted to the ★ **Ermita de Sant Miquel**. A short drive leads up to this pilgrimage chapel, built during the 19th century. It contains a magnificent high altar with the statues of Sant Miquel and Sant Joan. Next to the chapel there is a very good restaurant with a pleasant terrace.

About 37km (22 miles) into the trip between Montuïri and Vilafranca de Bonany, follow the signs on the left to the estate of ★ **Els Calderers de Sant Joan**. It is typical of the estates to be found on the plain of Mallorca. Built in 1750, it was a successful wine-growing centre until the advent of phylloxera in 1870, employing around 40 labourers. Later the emphasis shifted from wine to cereal cultivation. The manor house, with its courtyard, garden, outbuildings and magnificent interior, has been open to the public since 1993. The guided tour leads through the various rooms of the main building, then through the wine cellar and the chapel. The granary is impressive, as is the typically Mallorcan kitchen with its various utensils. The outbuildings include a smithy, a wash-house, a bakery and a carpentry workshop.

In the lower section of the park, accommodated in cages or compounds, are over 15 different species of animal indigenous to the island.

The next town on the route is **Vilafranca de Bonany** (pop. 2,000), a fruit and vegetable centre. This is the place to buy those delicious little tomatoes still on their stalks (*tomàtigues de ramellet*), sweet peppers, apricots and melons. Vilafranca is particularly known for its honeydew melons, and there is a Melon Festival (*Festa de Meló*) on the second Sunday in September each year. In the town centre is the large 17th-century church of Santa Barbara. Vilafranca was also the birthplace of the writer and theologian Josep Nicolau Bauzà (1916–93), abbot of Lluc Monastery from 1957 to 1960.

Ripe for the festival

Drive back in the direction of Palma, and after about 1½km (1 mile) take the turn-off on the right signposted to **Sant Joan** (pop. 1,700), a town founded by the Moors. Its church of **Sant Joan Baptista** dates back to 1293 and has a magnificent interior, with an alabaster pulpit and a valuable panelled ceiling. Above the town is the ★ **Santuari de la Consolació**, containing a statue of the Virgin. Legend has it that the statue was once found under a burning thorn bush by a young Arab boy, and the story is depicted in bright colours in a painting in the chapel. The *Festa des Butifarró* takes place in Sant Joan each year on the first Sunday in October, and there's a lot of good food available, including what for some people is probably an acquired taste – the famous Mallorcan black pudding (*butifarró*), from which the festival takes its name.

57

Windmill in Sineu

From Sant Joan it's 7km (4 miles) or so to ★ **Sineu** (pop. 2,500), referred to as Sinium in the writings of Pliny. During the Moorish occupation the town was one of the most important on the island, and under James II it became

Sineu was once a royal town

the summer residence of the Mallorcan royal family. Sineu is at the geographical centre of the island, and is famous today for its weekly market held in the central square every Wednesday. The market square is dominated by the large church of ★ **Mare de Déu dels Angels**, built in 1248. The magnificent interior boasts silver candelabra, stained-glass windows, 17th-century paintings and a valuable collection of monstrances and gold crucifixes. The Lion of St Mark – representing the town's patron saint – has stood in the Plaça de Sant Marc since 1945. *Sa Fira*, the island's largest cattle and craft market, is held here on 1 May each year. The town hall is in the Carrer Sant Francesc, and parts of it surround the cloister of the neighbouring church. Many old *cellers* (converted wine cellars serving typical Mallorcan cuisine, *see Food and Drink, page 89*) are found in this part of the town.

It's hard to miss the piece of modern sculpture spanning the road next to the former railway station on the outskirts of Sineu. The station building dates from 1878, and used to be on the Inca to Artà line which was closed down in 1975. In 1988 Klaus Drobig, a German artist, opened his ★ **S'Estacio art centre** in the disused FEVE station (Monday to Saturday 9.30am–1.30pm and 4–7pm, Saturday 9.30am–1pm, closed Sunday). He organises around six exhibitions a year, featuring the works of some 50 artists. A stroll around the station building is a rewarding experience. The ticket vendor at the entrance is a laughing Buddha, and alongside the numerous watercolours and drawings there are also several *pensiamentos* (thoughts) written down in German, Spanish or Mallorquí. Behind the building on the old platform there are several tables and chairs where visitors can sit and chat over a drink.

Directly opposite the station is the Foc i Terra exhibition building, containing ceramics, glass and sculpture.

S'Estacio art centre

Sweet delights in Inca

Almost halfway between Palma in the south and Alcúdia in the north is the town of ★ **Inca** (pop. 20,000), the third-largest on the island. It was an important town as far back as Roman times, and retained its significance during the Moorish occupation. Today, Inca is a centre of Mallorca's leather industry.

At the centre of the town is the church of **Santa Maria la Major**, with its free-standing campanile. The first church on the site was built in the 13th century, and was subjected to several alterations during the 18th and 19th centuries. The 17th-century monastery of **Sant Domènec** is also worth a visit. Inca's town hall is on the Plaça Espanya, as is the **Café Mercantil**, reckoned to be among the best of the island's coffee-houses. Its inviting interior, full of comfortable chairs upholstered in green leather, is hard to resist. At the bar there's a fine assortment of *tapas*

(*see Food and Drink, page 89*). Those with a sweet tooth should head for Can Delante in the Carrer Major, and its celebrated assortment of cakes and chocolates. Inca is also famous for its *cellers* (*see Food and Drink, page 89*).

Outside Celler Can Amer

The 14th-century hermitage of ★ **Santa Magdalena**, 6km (3¾ miles) away from the town on the Puig d'Inca (304m/997ft), makes a good detour at this point. There is a viewing terrace at the top and also a restaurant.

Just beyond Inca on the main road in the direction of Palma (C713) is the **Foro de Mallorca**, a wax museum with more than 50 wax figures and also several staged scenes from the island's history; the Archduke Ludwig Salvator (*see page 38*) is one of the latest additions (1994). Next to the museum there is a water amusement park, and a mini golf course.

The next town on the route is ★ **Binissalem** (pop. 4,674), in the heart of the wine-growing area to the southwest of Inca. The name is Moorish in origin and means 'son of peace'. The wine region here includes the neighbouring towns of Consell and Santa Maria, and covers an area of around 600ha (1,480 acres). The big wine festival known as the Festa des Fermar takes place at the end of September. The church of La Asunció dates from the 13th century and contains a fine Madonna by Adrià Ferran. There is a memorial in honour of the local vintners outside the church. The **cemetery** at Binissalem is also worth a visit – it's one of the oldest on the island.

59

The town of **Santa Maria del Camí** (pop. 4,000) also dates back to the days of the Moorish occupation. There was a thriving settlement here as long ago as Roman times. Step through the large entrance portal of the **Can Conrado**, a 17th-century mansion on the main street through the town, and enter the quiet cloister of the former convent of **Los Minimos**. Unfortunately, the history museum at the rear of the building is closed at present. Near the turn-off in the direction of Bunyola is a 17th-century fountain with a wooden water wheel (*sini*) formerly turned by a mule with blinkers. Those looking for authentic craftwork should visit the ceramic workshop Ceràmica Can Bernat in the Carrer Bartolomeu Pasqual, or Textiles Bujosa at Carrer Bernardo de Santa Eugenia 77 (on the main road to Palma).

Los Minimos and its cloister

The little town of **Alaró** (pop. 3,645) lies at the foot of the rocky outcrop of the same name on the road leading to Orient. It can be reached from Santa Maria del Camí either via Consell, or by taking the road to Bunyola and then turning right. Many of the local population make their living in the shoe and textile industries. On the main square is the town hall with its arcades and the church of Sant Bartomeu, which dates back to the 13th century. Above the altar is the Virgen del Refugio, a copy of which is kept in the chapel on the hill next to the ★★ **Castell d'Alaró**. The road to this ruined castle is signposted, and begins just outside the town. It first leads across gentle landscape, but the final stretch is not advisable for vehicles without four-wheel drive as the road surface suddenly becomes a furrowed track. The best thing is to park before this section begins. At the Bar Es Pouet (parking available) the ascent on foot takes at least another 30 minutes.

View from Castell d'Alaró

The Castell d'Alaró was built during the Moorish occupation of Mallorca, and the Moors managed to hold on to it even after the island was recaptured by James I of Aragon in 1229. It was only in 1289 that the lords of the castle, Cabrit and Bassa, were finally forced to surrender to the troops of King Alphonse III. They were duly burned at the stake. The castle terrace, 822m (2,696ft) up, provides a stunning panoramic ★★ **view** of the entire island. Next to the chapel of Nostra Senyora del Refugio there is a small restaurant. Simple accommodation is also available.

A paradise for climbers

On the left-hand side of the road, roughly 2km (1 mile) before the village of Orient comes into view, a hiking path branches off in the direction of the Castell d'Alaró, and on the right-hand side 200m (650ft) further on is one of the finest hotels on the island, L'Hermitage (*see Accommodation, page 102*).

Sleepy Orient

The sleepy mountain village of ★ **Orient** (pop. 20) has a handful of stone houses, a hotel and three restaurants. The fact that accommodation is readily available here makes Orient an ideal base for walking tours of the region. One good hiking destination is the 10-km (6-mile) long Apple Valley, studded with apricot and cherry trees and flocks of grazing sheep.

Orient's 20 or so inhabitants live in houses grouped round the hill with the church on top, the **Església de Sant Jordi** (consecrated to the village's patron saint). The church has a fine baroque altar with a statue of the Virgin and to look around it, the key can be obtained at the presbytery. The church and the village school next to it can be reached via the flight of steps known as Reis d'Orient. Here, a series of painted tiles depict St George fighting a hilarious-looking dragon.

Travel via Bunyola now (*see page 42*) to return straight to Palma.

Route 6

Tiny harbours and large country towns

Palma – Llucmajor – Santanyí – Cala Figuera – Ses
Salines – Colònia de Sant Jordi – Sa Ràpita –
S'Estanyol – Capocorb Vell – Cap Blanc – S'Arenal
– Palma (121km/75 miles) *See map on pages 44–5*

In the morning the busy markets in the typical Mallorcan country towns of Llucmajor and Campos are definitely
worth a visit. The highlight of the church of Sant Julià
in Campos is Murillo's painting of *Sant Crist de la Paciència*. The route then continues via the peaceful town of Santanyí to the picturesque fishing village and holiday resort
of Cala Figuera. Those keen on horticulture will enjoy a
stroll around the Botanicactus garden near Ses Salines.
A relaxing bathe and then lunch can be enjoyed either at
the holiday resort of Colònia de Sant Jordi, the beach of
Es Trenc or the small village of Sa Ràpita.

Market day

The high point of this route is a visit to the prehistoric
settlement of Capocorb Vell. From there it's not far to Cap
Blanc with its lighthouse and superb view as far as the
island of Cabrera. The trip back to Palma goes through
lonely pine forests at some distance from the coast. From
Son Verí onwards, though, this tranquillity is shattered:
the hotels belonging to the busy tourist centres of S'Arenal, Las Maravillas and Can Pastilla appear along the extensive Platja de Palma, which stretches all the way to
the island's capital.

61

Capocorb Vell

Leave Palma on the motorway towards S'Arenal and then
follow the C717 as far as ★★ **Llucmajor** (pop. 17,000).
There was a settlement here even before the Christians
took the island. The town was raised to the status of a villa
by James III in 1300; and at the beginning of this century it was given its royal charter by King Alphonse XIII.
From 1916 onwards, the railway stopped in Llucmajor,
making it easy to reach Palma and the sea. When the railway station at S'Arenal was opened, tourism began. The
James III Esplanade, with a statue at the end of it of the
king who fell near Llucmajor, leads to the town centre.

Llucmajor has remained largely untouched by modern tourism. At its centre is the Plaça Espanya with the
Casa Consistorial (town hall), built in 1882. This trian-
gular square has several shady benches, and some good
coffee-houses too, notably the Café Colón, which dates
from 1928. Just around the corner is the fish market hall,
originally built in 1915 and modernised in 1986. The small
building is made of huge blocks of stone and has several
pretty wrought-iron sections painted blue. Directly next

to it is the **church of San Miquel**, first mentioned as early as 1248. The present building dates from the 18th century.

At the junction of the Carrer Bisbe Taxaquet and the Carrer Antonio Maura, a few metres away from the esplanade, a monument to Mallorca's cobblers, erected in 1985, can be seen in the middle of a small square. Many of the inhabitants of Llucmajor were employed in the flourishing shoe industry until comparatively recently, and a lot of the shoes produced here are still exported. Most people work in the service sector today, although a small percentage are employed in agriculture. Almond and apricot plantations can be found in the region surrounding the town.

Local observer

Also in the Carrer Bisbe Taxaquet is the former **Hotel España**, which was opened in 1916 and formerly provided accommodation for businessmen and travelling salesmen. The facade has some fine art nouveau details. Friday is market day here, and in mid-October the agricultural fair known as the *Feria Campesina de Llucmajor* takes place, accompanied by several cultural events. The town has many music groups, as well as a folk-dancing group. On the edge of the town is an old mill that has recently been renovated, and the restaurant next door to it, Es Molí dén Gaspar, is definitely worth a visit.

Small is beautiful

The friendly country town of **Campos** lies at the centre of an agricultural region full of wind machines that scoop up water for irrigation. It was founded by James II in the year 1300. There had already been a Moorish settlement on the site, and coins dating from Roman times have been discovered during archaeological digs. If rumours are to be believed there are still several Roman ships lying on the sea bed off the coast here. The **church of Sant Julià** was originally built in 1248 and the present building dates from the 19th century. The highlight inside is the famous painting of ★★ **Sant Crist de la Paciència**, a work by the Seville painter Bartolomé Esteban Murillo (1617–82). It was painted in the mid-17th century and then found its way to Campos in 1800. Today it hangs in a side chapel, decorated by architect Miguel Alcover; the gate is by Antoni Prohens. Permission to visit the church and its Museu Parroquial must be obtained from the Rectoría. One curiosity of the museum is its large collection of offertory bowls with figures of saints.

Another church worth visiting is **San Blas**, a Gothic structure built after the Christian victory in 1229 and situated some distance outside the centre. The town hall on the Plaça Major in Campos dates from 1642. From the 15th to the 16th centuries, the town received a complicated system of fortifications, with watchtowers connected to each other by tunnels. Six of these towers can still be seen.

The magnificent palazzi in the town centre include Sa Creu, in front of which the weekly market is held. Campos is especially busy on market days (Thursday and Saturday). A regional speciality is capers, which are harvested between June and August each year. Those with a sweeter tooth should visit the Can Pomar confectionery shop, at Carrer de la Creu 20.

Returning with the catch,
Cala Figuera

63

The peaceful inland town of **Santanyí** is the administrative centre for the districts of Cala Figuera, Cala Santanyí and S'Alqueria Blanca. South of the town, beside the road signposted to Ses Salines, a huge cistern, which used to contain water for horses to drink, lies in the middle of a well-tended park. The gate of Sa Porta Murada is all that remains of a powerful system of fortifications which protected Santanyí against frequent pirate raids during the Middle Ages.

The Plaça Major is dominated by the large 18th-century church of Sant Andreu Apòstel, with the small 13th-century Capilla del Roser behind it. The church itself contains a famous organ built by Jordi Bosch which can be seen by asking for the key from the presbytery. Next door is the new Bar Sa Cova (Plaça Major 30), a non-smoking café which serves good home-made cakes. There's some excellent craftwork to be admired at Ceràmiques de Santanyí (Carrer Guardia Civil 22), a small workshop run as a family business since 1979 and producing ceramics according to its own special designs, some decorated with traditional Mallorcan patterns.

The route now continues from Santanyí across some very attractive landscape, as far as the coast and ★★ **Cala Figuera**. A *cala* is a small bay (*bahia* is larger), and can be sandy or rocky, covered with gravel, or just a tiny, protected harbour for fishing boats, like Cala Figuera.

Cala Figuera: Bon Bar Café

The idyllic harbour

It's a quiet little place, even though most of the holiday-makers here are young. The fishing boats lie side by side along the rim of the tiny bay, and there is a walk around the edges of two fjord-like inlets – Caló d'en Boire and Caló d'en Busques – to reach the lighthouse and the Torre d'en Bèu. In this picturesque little harbour the fishing nets are regularly inspected for holes and laid out to dry in front of the building belonging to the Confraria de Pescadors (fishermen's fraternity). Cala Figuera has retained its romantic flair despite tourism, which is one reason why people keep coming back every year. Those wishing to swim usually go to the sandy beaches nearby such as Caló Mondrago to the north, or the bays of Cala Santanyí and Cala Llombarts to the south. Cala Figuera is particularly popular with German visitors.

Prickly pear in Botanicactus

Travel via Santanyí now along the side-road leading to **Ses Salines**. Just before the village comes into view, take a turn-off to the right. Here, in the grounds of the Finca Camp de Sa Creu, is ★★ **Botanicactus** (daily summer 9am–7.30pm, winter 9.30am–4.30pm), one of the largest botanical gardens in Europe. Opened in 1989, it covers an area of 150,000sq m (178,000sq yd) and contains around 1,600 different species of plant, 120 of them from the Mediterranean region. The park has been divided up into three sections: the large marshland section contains the biggest artificial lake in the Balearic archipelago, surrounded by palm trees; the cactus garden has 400 different varieties including several species of agave; and the so-called Mallorcan garden has olive, almond, pine and orange trees, as well as a stunning assortment of flowers. A network of paths runs through the park, which boasts sparrows and finches up in the trees, and swans and ducks on the lake. The garden centre is the latest addition.

Situated on the rocky promontory of Sa Puntassa, and flanked by the little islands of Na Corbarana, Na Guardis, des Cabots, des Frares and many others, **Colònia de Sant Jordi** is a resort area that's still growing. Archaeological excavations have resulted in the discovery of the first ever Phoenician settlement on Mallorca. Once Colònia de Sant Jordi was the fishing harbour of Campos with just a handful of huts, today it's a mass of hotels and apartment complexes.

Down in the harbour, tickets to the island of Cabrera can be purchased from a small booth next door to the visitor centre for the Parc Nacional de Cabrera, which provides hiking maps and information on the flora and fauna of the island. At the centre of the town is the modern church, built in 1972, with its free-standing campanile. To the east, next to the yachting harbour, is the sandy beach of Els Dolç, and past the last hotels to the west is the nudist beach of Es Trenc (*see page 66*).

Fun on the beach

★★ **Cabrera** is the fifth of the Balearic Islands. The archipelago off the Cap de Ses Salines, with its 12 islands and total surface area of 17sq km (6½ sq miles), is an extension of the Serra de Llevant mountain range. The islands lie to the south of Colònia de Sant Jordi, and the largest of them measures 7km (4¼ miles) by 5km (3 miles). The coast of Cabrera is rocky and the centre is rugged, with limestone hills reaching elevations of 170m (557ft). The two bays, Port de Cabrera and Cala Ganduf, serve as natural harbours, and are popular with yachts in the summertime – those planning to anchor here, though, need a permit in advance from the nature conservation authorities, because only a certain number of boats are allowed.

During the Napoleonic Wars, Cabrera was used as a prison island where over 5,000 Frenchmen died of hunger between 1809 and 1813. The island has no village, only barracks inhabited by Spanish soldiers. Cabrera is part of a restricted area, and has been a nature reserve since 1991. A popular hiking route leads up to the castle 72m (236ft) above the sea.

From Colònia Sant Jordi the journey continues past the extensive salt-works of **Es Salobrar**. The salt from this basin has been placed in a huge mound by the firm of Salinas de Levante SA. Many migratory birds rest here in the autumn on their way southwards. The route then continues onwards in the direction of Campos, and soon the **Banys de Sant Joan de Sa Fonta Santa** (Baths of St John) come into view. Today's bath-house was opened in 1845, but the healing power of the waters here has been well-known since antiquity. Rheumatism, arthritis and bronchitis can all be treated at these thermal baths.

Just beyond the thermal baths, the route continues along a minor road in the direction of La Ràpita. Before the yacht harbour appears, a small side road leads off to the left to the beach of **Es Trenc** and the little community of Ses Covetes. The name literally means 'small caves', and refers to the numerous caves in the vicinity that were used as burial chambers by the Romans. During the late 19th century, several families from Campos built their summer houses on the rocky plateau, though no hotels were erected.

Out of season, Es Trenc used to be very popular with beachcombers, and deckchair rental firms did quite good business despite the lack of hotels. The beach has long been popular with naturists, even during the Franco era, and the people of Ses Covetes used to provide their visitors with simple food. Recently, at the Ses Covetes end of the beach, the idyll has been disrupted by the construction of new holiday complexes, and work even began on a 68-storey apartment block. However, there is some hope that these developments will not be allowed to get out of hand. Further work has been stopped for the time being as environmentalists and other local pressure groups have taken the matter to court.

The two holiday resorts of **Sa Ràpita** and **S'Estanyol** have almost grown into one community. Originally they were just a collection of fishermen's huts and boathouses. Then wealthy families from Llucmajor built their first summer houses along this strip of the coast, and in 1870 a yacht club was founded in S'Estanyol. A few years later the yachting harbour of Sa Ràpita was built next to the old watchtower, which dates from 1595. Both resorts are eerily deserted during the winter months, especially on weekdays, but in summer there's quite a crowd, and the seafood restaurants along the coast road are often packed.

A coastline worth preserving

The next destination is the prehistoric settlement of
★★ **Capocorb Vell** (daily except Thursday 10am–5pm),
the best-known Bronze Age site on Mallorca. The first
excavations here were carried out between 1910 and 1920
under the supervision of the archaeologist Josep Colom-
inas Roca, and the area has been open to the public since
1953. The buildings of the former settlement lie within
a Cyclopean wall, and the entire prehistoric village can be
inspected by means of a well-organised system of paths.
The foundations of 28 impressively large buildings can be
seen; the entrances to several of them still have stones
across the top. The remains of pillars can also be observed
in a number of the inner rooms. At the edge of the village there are two massive square *talayots* and three round
megalithic towers.

Dwellings at Capocorb Vell

Drive on from Capocorb Vell to the remote and idyllic bay
of ★ **Cala Pi**. On this promontory, next to the San Miguel
restaurant, there is a funnel-shaped, 17th-century watchtower. From here, the white sandy beach of Es Trenc and
the high-rise hotels at Colònia de Sant Jordi can be seen
across to the left, and to the right some steps lead down
to the bay of Cala Pi with its pine forest at the centre.
The newly built apartment complex called Cala Pi Club is
probably going to rob this little bay of some of its tranquillity, and parking spaces around the San Miguel restaurant are increasingly hard to find during the summer
months. The resort of Cala Pi is right next to the holiday
village of Vallgomera.

67

The rocky promontory with the lighthouse on top called
★★ **Cap Blanc** lies at the foot of Palma Bay and has a view
extending as far as the island of Cabrera. Down below
the little fishing boats can be seen sailing slowly by. The
rocks around this lighthouse are an ideal place for a picnic high above the sea. The distance from the Cap Blanc
lighthouse to S'Arenal is 17km (10 miles); the route lies
at some distance from the coast, and leads through thorny
scrub and pretty pine forests. The little road with its stone
walls has hardly any traffic at all to begin with, but grows
a lot busier as it nears Palma Bay.

The route passes through the villa suburb of Son Verí, with
its fine views of Palma Bay, before arriving at the yachting harbour of **S'Arenal** and the old quarter of the town,
where a handful of fishermen's houses have survived the
onslaught of tourism. S'Arenal is where the long strip of
coastline known as the Playa de Palma begins, and from
here to the island's capital the coast road is crammed with
high-rise hotels right next to the beach. It continues via
Can Pastilla before reaching Palma.

Route 7

Castles, caves and hermitages

Cala Rajada – Capdepera – Artà – Manacor – Felanitx – Cala d'Or – Porto Colom – Porto Cristo – Cala Millor – Cala Rajada (123km/78 miles) *See map on pages 44–5*

The harbour at Cala Rajada

Cala Rajada, once a fishing village, still has a charming harbour, and is the starting point for this route. Not far away from it are the fortified towns of Capdepera and Artà, dominated by the battlements of their mighty fortresses. Picturesque town centres and many historic buildings lend these towns a special charm. Near Artà, the prehistoric settlement of Ses Païses can be visited, or there's an optional detour northwards to the Ermita de Betlem. The next stop on the route is the industrial town of Manacor, where the famous Mallorcan artificial pearls are manufactured. The journey then continues across the southern foothills of the Serra de Levant to the wine-producing town of Felanitx. The holy mountain of Sant Salvador and the castle rock of Santueri are two of the highlights here. The route then carries on towards the coast, to the holiday resort of Cala d'Or, known for its Ibiza-style architecture.

The trip back to Cala Rajada follows along the coast and leads past Porto Cristo with its limestone caverns, and Cala Millor with its Reserva Africana wildlife reserve. Another interesting sight along the route is the Torre de Canyamel, a huge square watchtower high above the sea and surrounded by magnificent scenery. The caverns of Artà are quite close by, and make a worthwhile detour.

Cala Rajada, at the northeasternmost point of Mallorca, is the most important fishing harbour on the island after Palma, it forms part of the municipal district of Capdepera, and has become an important centre of tourism in recent years. Despite the large number of hotels, the town is still surprisingly relaxed, and accommodation is both cheap and comfortable.

Several footpaths lead through shady pine forests via the small Cala Gat to the lighthouse up on the 48-m (157-ft) high **Punta des Faralló**, or to the neighbouring beaches of Cala Agulla, Cala Moltó (both naturist), or Cala Mesquida with its beautiful dunes. The Platja de Son Moll to the south can be reached via the beach promenade, lined with cafés, bars and restaurants. Still further south is the bay known as **Sa Font de Sa Cala**, named after a nearby freshwater spring that flows directly into the sea. The beaches at Cala Agulla, Son Moll and Font de Sa Cala are connected by a miniature railway.

Above the harbour is Cala Rajada's most famous building, the villa **Sa Torre Cega**, built in 1911 by the wealthy March family of bankers, and surrounded by an impressive ★★ **sculpture park**. The park was laid out by the English garden architect Russell Page and covers an area of 60,000 sq m (71,750 sq yd). It contains several abstract sculptures, including works by Henry Moore and Auguste Rodin, and there are also works by contemporary Spanish artists, including *In Praise of Architecture* by the Basque sculptor Eduardo Chillida. The *Serenates d'Estiu* festival of classical music and song is held here in the grounds of the Villa March in July each year. On 16 July the local fishermen have a fiesta in honour of their patron saint, St Carmen, and on 16 August the town's patron saint, St Roc, is also honoured with processions at sea.

Traditional headgear

About 3 km (1¾ miles) inland from Cala Rajada is the town of ★★ **Capdepera**. Its ochre-coloured houses are clustered together at the foot of a massive medieval fortress, the largest in Mallorca (daily 1 April to 30 September 10am–8pm, 1 October to 31 March 10am–5pm). The origins of the fortress date back to Roman times, then the Moors enlarged it and the Christians strengthened it still further under James II. The entire structure was renovated at the beginning of the 1980s. A flight of steps leads up to it from the Plaça Espanya and the Torre de Sa Baira leads into the main section, with the renovated Casa del Gobernador and the Capilla de la Esperança, both commissioned by King Sanxo at the beginning of the 14th century. There is a superb view across the countryside from the rooms inside the fortress.

69

The fortress of Capdepera

Below the defensive wall is the **church of Sant Bartomeu**, built during the last century; it contains the Madonna statue known as Nostra Senyora de la Esperança. The statue was in the fortress chapel for many years, and according to legend it helped the lords of the castle during a pirate raid. Apparently a sudden fog descended, and the terrified attackers were forced to retreat. The Café Orient in the small Plaça d'Orient is a nice coffee-house to while away some time in, and the winding streets of the town still contain several artisans' workshops where hats, baskets and mats are still made according to time-honoured techniques.

The battlements of Artà

Although the name of the town of **Artà** is Moorish in origin, it actually dates back to the Bronze Age. Today this historic little town lies beneath the battlements of its fortress, and proudly bears a castle on its coat of arms. On the Plaça d'Espanya, which is more like a park than a square, the ★ **Museu Regional d'Artà** (municipal museum) can be seen next to the Casa Consistorial (town hall), restored in 1941. The museum is housed inside the same palazzo as the Sa Nostra bank, and contains archaeological finds dating from Phoenician, Greek and Roman times; there is also a natural science collection and an ethnological department.

Another sight worth seeing is the church of **Transfiguració del Senyor**, first mentioned as early as the 13th century (the priest will be happy to show you around, but remember to put something in his collection box). The large rose window above the main portal is very impressive, as is the carved wooden pulpit. Beyond the church, a broad flight of steps flanked by cypress trees and stone crosses leads up to the fortress and to the ★★ **Santuari de Sant Salvador d'Artà**. There is a fine view from the

Artà fortress...

top of the hill of the jumble of houses below and of the fertile plain surrounding the town. The view from up here extends as far as Canyamel on the east coast.

...and the town below

The fortress was built in the 13th century on the remains of an earlier Moorish structure, and its inner courtyard, with its benches, palm trees and fountains, is a tranquil retreat. The pilgrimage church contains some impressive paintings on various themes, including the martyrdom of the Catalan mystic Ramón Llull, and the defeat of the Moors by James I. There is also a painting of St Anthony. The church is completely enclosed by a battlemented wall, with round and square watchtowers along it. A small shop next to the church sells drinks and postcards. St Anthony, the patron saint of pet animals, has a special significance here in Artà; on 16 January the townsfolk celebrate Sant Antoni Abat with a procession, and on 13 June the Sant Antoni de Juny festival is held. The latter dates back to the foundation of the Franciscan monastery in 1581. Part of the festivities involve the famous Cavallet, the small papier-mâché horse that the dancers strap round their hips. There is also a classical music festival in the summer, with concerts in local churches.

71

An interesting alternative route at this point is a visit to the *talayot* settlement of ★ **Ses Païses**, which can be reached along the tracks of the former railway (signposted). There is a well-shaded car park at the entrance, from which a path leads to the Cyclopean wall surrounding the prehistoric settlement. The wall has an impressive entrance gateway. The ruins include several square foundations and also a *talayot* with a small chamber at its base. There is also a striking naveta-shaped (oval) room containing the remains of several pillars. Unfortunately the settlement is in a state of disrepair and badly damaged. The stones from the walls have been used by farmers as construction material, and some of the buildings provide makeshift accommodation for sheep, pigs and goats.

Prehistoric remains at Ses Païses

Another possible detour is the ★ **Ermita de Betlem**. Even if this small pilgrimage church happens to be closed, the trip itself is worth it just for the superb scenery on the way. The road passes green fields, fig and olive trees, sheep pastures and pine forests, and follows the course of a mountain stream. Several rather modest-looking farmhouses are passed along the way too. Even before arrival at the hermitage itself there are some fine views to be had of the north coast, down to the holiday resort of Colònia de Sant Pere and, in good weather, as far as the Cap de Formentor and across to the neighbouring island of Menorca. The last section of the route is full of hairpins and is reminiscent of the notorious Sa Calobra stretch on the northwest

Making pearls in Manacor

coast (*see page 47–8*). A path leads down to the coast (Colònia de Sant Pere) from the pilgrimage chapel. The hermitage was founded in 1805, and consecrated in 1806 by Cardinal Despuig. The church's dome contains some interesting frescoes and several of the hermits lie buried in the small churchyard.

Halfway between Artà and Manacor is the small town of **Sant Llorenç des Cardassar** (pop. 5,000). This pleasant little market town is the administrative centre for the district of the same name, to which part of the holiday resort of Cala Millor also belongs. The first church here was built in around 1236 but today's structure dates from the mid-17th century. The left-hand side chapel contains the statue of the Mare de Déu Trobada.

The coat of arms of the town of **Manacor** (pop. 25,000) shows a hand (*man*) on a heart (*cor*), and indeed the heart of this town is something the bus tourists never see when they come to visit the pearl factories out in the suburbs. Manacor dates back to Roman times, and the Moors had a settlement here too. Today this industrial town, with its pearl and furniture factories, is the second largest on the island. The market hall on the Plaça de la Constitució has absolutely everything; the bakeries sell Manacor's special *suspiros* biscuits; and after all the busy shopping the church of ★ **Dolors de Nostra Senyora** is a good place to sit down and unwind. It has a Gothic ribbed vault, and an 84-m (275-ft) high campanile.

An attractive souvenir

The streets directly behind the church hold several architectural surprises in store, such as the building occupied by the Banco de Credito Balear (Carrer d'en Bosch on the corner of Juan Segura), an old apothecary with stained-glass windows (Carrer Juan Segura 12), or the exhibition hall of the Banca March (Carrer Major 21). Walk past the attractive facades along the Carrer Major and soon the Plaça del Convento comes into view, with its former Dominican monastery plus two-storeyed baroque cloister. Don't be surprised at how busy the place looks as today it contains several offices belonging to the municipal authorities. The church of ★ **Cristo Rey** has some good frescoes inside, and the church of San Vicente Ferrer, once part of the Dominican monastery, contains a fine Churriguera-style baroque altarpiece.

On the edge of Manacor's old town is the **Torre de Ses Puntes**, part of the former fortifications. It has been a listed national monument since 1925. The Torre dels Enegistes was also part of the old wall, and today houses the town's **Archaeological Museum** (Tuesday to Thursday 10am–1pm). Exhibits include a prehistoric collection and several fragments of mosaics taken from the Roman-Christian basilica of Son Peretó. Part of the building is taken up by an exhibition hall with works of modern art and sculpture. The S'Agricola art association in the Plaça Sa Bassa also has a number of modern paintings and sculptures on display.

73

Don't leave Manacor without visiting a ★ **pearl factory** – Majorica (Via Roma 48–52) is the best-known. Majorica imitation pearls are created via a complex procedure involving fish scales and essence of mother-of-pearl and can hardly be distinguished from the real thing.

Sites such as the prehistoric settlement of **Clossos de Can Gaià** with its *talayots* and burial chambers have now made it clear that the area around the town of ★ **Felanitx** (pop. 15,000) was populated as long ago as the Bronze Age. Today this wine town can look back on a successful past as an important centre of trade and industry, which has a reputation of producing the best brains in Mallorca. A long list of Mallorcan politicians, writers, architects and intellectuals are proud Felanitxers; the internationally celebrated young painter Miquel Barceló (*see page 85*) was also born here. The slopes around the town contain not only vineyards but also apricot and orange plantations.

Those heading for the Carrer Major or the town hall will not fail to miss the huge ★ **church of Sant Miquel**, first mentioned in 1248 and renovated in the mid-18th century. It stands majestically at the top of an inviting flight of steps. The interior is just as grand, with candelabra, votive lamps and carved altarpieces in the side chapels, velvet drapes, a massive high altar and an enormous organ. Outside on the main facade, between the portal and the rose window, the archangel Michael stands on the head of the devil in chains. The broad baroque facade – one of the finest on the island – is dominated by a square bell tower.

Sant Miquel in Felanitx

Opposite the church is the Plaça Sa Font de Santa Margalida. Some steps lead down into an oval crypt containing a public fountain dating from 1830. The attractive patrician's house on the square, **Can Prohens**, contains an arts centre. Behind the church is the Casa Consistorial (town hall) with its large arches and the spacious market hall. On the broad esplanades around the town centre are several excellent coffee-houses, such as the Café Can Moix (Carrer Guillem Timoner 1).

Christ at Santuari de Sant Salvador

A detour from Felanitx that should not be missed is a trip to the ★★★ **Santuari de Sant Salvador**, one of Mallorca's most important hermitages, perched on a rock 509m (1,669ft) above sea level. It was built in 1348, then a second church was built on the site in 1595, and today's structure dates from 1734. On one side of the hill is a huge 14-m (45-ft) high **stone cross**, and on the other the monument to Cristo Rei (1934), a 7-m (22-ft) high statue of Christ with crown and sceptre. The monastery church contains a fine alabaster retable showing scenes from the Passion and the Last Supper. It is thought to have been carved in around 1500, and is the only example of stonemasonry on Mallorca. The viewing terraces here afford some of the best views of the island, and beneath the church there are some pleasantly shady picnic sites. Pilgrims and visitors can also be accommodated here in the 13 cells.

The stone cross

Castell de Santueri

South of Felanitx is the famous ★★ **Castell de Santueri** (Easter to 31 October 10am–7pm). From the turn-off 2km (1¼ miles) out of Felanitx it's only another 5km (3 miles) or so. There's a car park beneath the walls where a flight of steps leads up to the entrance gate of the castle, which is 408m (1,338ft) above sea level. There were probably fortifications here as long ago as Roman times. The Moors then used the castle until it was surrendered to James I in 1230. The castle has had a surprisingly peaceful past, and was mostly used as a place of refuge from pirate attacks as the coast could also be observed. Although King Ferdinand of Aragon ordered the castle to be abandoned in 1484, the Mallorcans continued to use it. In 1596, when the English plundered Cadiz, the resulting panic led the women and children in Felanitx to take refuge up here. The view from the north side of the castle, with its impressive wall, extends from the nearby wooded hills to the Puig de Sant Salvador.

Cala d'Or

The hotels and apartments in the holiday resort of **Cala d'Or** are snow-white and flat-roofed. The first of them appeared in the 1930s, and they were designed in the cube-shaped Ibizan style by the architect Pep Costa Ferrer (1876–1971). The sense of architectural unity here is impressive. The five sandy beaches nearby also form part of the resort, and there is a very elegant yacht harbour too. High above one of the bays is the former fortress of Es Fortí, recently restored and now open to the public. Life here during the summer is pretty noisy (discos, music bars, and so on).

The coastal resort of ★ **Porto Colom** just to the north of Cala d'Or was formerly the harbour town of Felanitx, 12km (7 miles) away. The view from the main road of its quiet bay and the Punta de Ses Crestes in the distance is formidable. Legend has it that Cristobal Colom (Christopher Columbus) was born on Mallorca, in Felanitx, which explains the name given to this harbour town. Despite all the construction work, Porto Colom still remains a very pleasant place. The few hotel complexes are all outside the town centre along the stretch of beach to the south. The coastline around the harbour bay with its tiny beaches is pretty and is rounded off by the lighthouse at the end.

Porto Colom

The stretch of road between Porto Colom and **Porto Cristo**, Manacor's former harbour, leads through some attractive pine forest. Today Porto Cristo is a busy beach resort and a popular tourist destination. The famous ★★ **dragon caves** (Coves del Drac) are the main draw here, so named because the people of Porto Cristo believed that a dragon lived in their depths.

75

The caves have been well-known since antiquity, and were first mentioned in 1338. The first map of the grottoes was drawn up in 1880, and the underground lake was first discovered at the end of the 19th century by the Frenchman Edouard Alfred Martel, who had been sent on a mission of exploration here by the Archduke Ludwig Salvator (*see page 38*). The **Lago Martel** is the largest subterranean lake in Europe, and is 177m (580ft) long,

Missing link in the dragon caves

up to 30m (98ft) wide and up to 8m (26ft) high. The brightly lit caverns have been made accessible to the public, and the route with its bridges and paths is around 2km (1¼ miles) long. The classical concerts held on the lake, with their clever lighting effects, are a highlight of any visit here. The huge stalactites and stalagmites add to the atmosphere, and after the concert the spectators are taken across the clear water of the lake in white boats (daily 10am–5pm, winter 10.45am–3.30pm).

Cala Millor

The strip of coastline around **Cala Millor** contains many *talayots*, burial mounds and burial chambers. Once a lonely stretch of dune-covered shoreline, this part of Mallorca has now developed into the most important resort area of eastern Mallorca. Cala Millor, Cala Bona and the Costa del Pins all lie on the 2-km (1¼-mile) long sandy beach of the bay of Son Severa, and south of the promontory of Punta de N'Amer are the resorts of Sa Coma and S'Illot. In fact the only section of coastline that hasn't been built up is the **Punta de N'Amer** itself, thanks to the intervention of local environmentalists. The nature reserve here covers an area of 200ha (500 acres) and the promontory also provides a good view of the surrounding coastline. At the centre of it is the **Castell de N'Amer**, a square, moated watchtower 10m (32ft) in height, built during the 17th century as a defence against pirates.

The ★★ **Reserva Africana** makes a good detour at this stage. It's a wildlife reserve south of Cala Millor, covering an area of 40ha (98 acres), with monkeys, antelopes, elephants, giraffes, rhinoceri and many other species of animal indigenous to Africa. They can either be observed from a safari mini-train that travels along 4km (2½ miles) of track, or from your own car. Baby animals can be observed in the compounds and cages of the baby zoo (daily 9am–7pm, winter 9am–4.30pm).

Torre de Canyamel

The scenic route between Cala Millor and Capdepera leads past the **Torre de Canyamel**, a square defensive tower dating from the 14th century built on Moorish foundations. Not far away is Platja Canyamel, with its gently sloping beach and tiny freshwater stream. Excursion boats leave from here in the summer for Cala Rajada.

The caverns known as the ★★ **Coves d'Artà** on Cap Vermell near Canyamel are 46m (150ft) above sea level, and were discovered by the French geologist Martel in 1876 (*see page 75*). A broad flight of steps leads up to the cavern entrance. So far 300m (1,000ft) of these caverns have been explored. A particularly famous stalagmite known as the 'Queen of Pillars' is 22m (72ft) high.

Route 8

The land of windmills

Port d'Alcúdia – Sa Pobla – Muro – Petra – Santa Margalida – Can Picafort – S'Albufera – Port d'Alcúdia (68km/42 miles) *See map on pages 44–5*

This route leads from the broad bay of Alcúdia across the flat, windmill-dotted landscape near the towns of Sa Pobla, Muro, Petra and Santa Margalida. Muro has an interesting ethnological museum, and Petra was the birthplace of the Mallorcan missionary Junípero Serra. The trip back goes via the small country town of Santa Margalida and the large holiday resort of Can Picafort. Beyond the miles of sandy beach in the bay of Alcúdia is the S'Albufera d'Alcúdia, a wide expanse of marshland. A walk or cycling tour in this area – the largest nature reserve in the Balearic archipelago – is the high spot of this route. Every autumn, bird-watchers come here from all over the world to observe migratory birds on their way south, but this nature reserve is a paradise for nature lovers at any time of year.

Travel along the multi-lane highway that cuts through the hotel zone of Alcúdia and take the narrow country road to ★ **Sa Pobla** directly after the Lago Grande. Follow this scenic little road for 9km (5½ miles) along the reed-covered banks of the Albufera marshlands. The Moorish settlement of Huayar Alfa was renamed Villa Real by James II after the Christian conquest, but until the 16th century was known by the Moorish-Christian name of Sa Pobla de Vialfás. It was only later that the town became Sa Pobla. The area was dry and agriculturally unproductive until the

Alcúdia beach

77

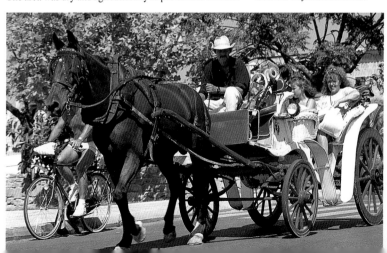

The slow way around Alcúdia

17th century, when a large part of the marshland north of it was reclaimed and sections were given to tenant farmers. Today the region around Sa Pobla is one of the most fertile on the island.

The town lies at the centre of the plain known as the 'land of a thousand windmills'. Mallorca's windmills are as characteristic of the island as its olive trees, and many of these wonders of medieval engineering have been restored and put back into use in recent years. This is particularly true of the fertile agricultural area around Sa Pobla, where potatoes are the number one export article.

The attractive main square of Sa Pobla has several fine old buildings, a town hall and the church consecrated to Sant Antoni Abat, the patron saint of pets. There has been a festival in his honour in Sa Pobla ever since the 14th century. On 16 January every year the locals light large bonfires, and there is much dancing and music. Everyone eats *espinagades* (pastries containing a mixture of sharply spiced vegetables and eel from the Albufera). On 17 January each year, the town's pets are led in a procession through the streets and then ritually blessed outside the church, to protect them from disease.

Local transport

The limestone caverns known as the ★ **Coves de Campanet** (daily 10am–6pm), just north of the village of the same name, are 6km (3¾ miles) away from Sa Pobla. The route there passes the small chapel of Sant Miquel, which has a fine statue of the Virgin on its altar. These caverns are not as spectacular as the Coves del Drac (*see page 75*) – there's no underground lake and no expensive light show – but they do contain the longest stalactite (3m/9ft) in the world. The caverns here at Campanet are normally visited by individuals rather than large groups.

Traditional windmill in Muro

The next town on the route, **Muro**, is 5km (3 miles) further on, along a straight section of country road that passes the estate of Son March. The first important date in Muro's history was 840, when the Moors turned the settlement of Algebelí into a charming town full of gardens. After the Christian conquest by James I the town became the property of Hugo Ponce, Count of Ampuries, the bishop of Gerona and the abbot of Sant Feliú de Guixols. The name of the town was changed to Muro, and in 1300 it was granted the status of a villa by James II. Muro is 117m (383ft) above sea level and lies at the centre of an agricultural area devoted to cereal and vegetables. The 16th-century **church of Sant Joan Baptista** has a fine free-standing square campanile, and inside the church there is an altar painting of St Michael by Joan Daurer. The town hall has a large stone balcony on its facade, and there is a leafy arcade on the ground floor.

The main attraction for most visitors to Muro, though, is its ★★ **Ethnological Museum** (Carrer Major 15, Tuesday to Saturday 10am–2pm and 4–7pm, Sunday 10am–2pm). The collection is housed inside an old palazzo and provides a good glimpse into traditional Mallorcan life. The exhibits include tools, agricultural implements, ceramics and also an apothecary. Other collections range from relics of the once famous spoon-making industry to an exhibition of old carriages. It is important to allow plenty of time for a visit here.

The route now joins the road to Manacor, 2km (1¼ miles) south of Santa Margalida and continues to the small town of **Petra** (pop. 2,700). The best place to leave the car here is in front of the church of Sant Pere. The gardens outside the church contain a memorial to the island's patron saint, Catalina Thomàs. Inside the building there is an interesting Gothic font, where in 1713 a farmer's son was baptised Miguel José, who grew up to be the Mallorcan missionary Fray Junípero Serra (1713–84). As a young boy he was accepted into Petra's Franciscan monastery of San Bernardino. Later he went to Palma and then left for North America as a Franciscan missionary. His trip there, which lasted 99 days, took him via Cadiz, the Canary Islands, Puerto Rico and Veracruz, Mexico. One of the 21 missions he founded developed into the Californian city of San Francisco, and many others also became large cities. His bust stands today among those of the great in the Capitol Building in Washington.

The ★ **museum** portraying Serra's life and work is well signposted. Turn off the Carrer Major into the Carrer Junípero Serra, which begins next to the church of San Bernardino and is decorated with pretty majolica tiles, each depicting the various missions founded by Serra. He was born at his grandparents' house, but since it no longer exists visitors are taken to Serra's parents' house in the Carrer Barracar Alt, a simple thatched cottage with a small yard where he grew up. The house was the property of the City of San Francisco for many years, but was made over to the Casa Serra Foundation in 1981. The museum adjacent to the Casa Serra was opened in 1955, and contains maps, sketches, letters, coins and also scale models and pictures of Serra's missions in California and Mexico. The 100-kilo bronze plaque is a present from the Mexican government. Serra spent a total of nine years in the Mexican town of Querétaro, and during that time he founded five missions. There is also a comprehensive library here. The key to the Casa Serra and to the museum can be obtained at Carrer P Miguel de Petra 2.

Junípero Serra and his museum

On Wednesdays in the Plaça Ramón Llull there is a pleasant fruit and vegetable market, observed by elderly

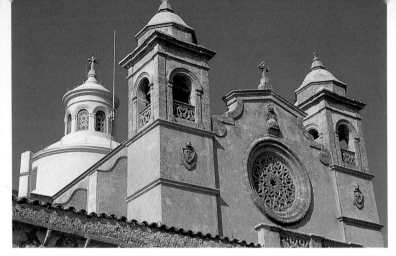

Nostra Senyora de Bonany

men of the town from seats in the shade outside the bar Can Tomeu. The nearby Plaça de Junípero Serra, with its statue of the missionary, is also a good place to relax.

A worthwhile detour can be made at this stage to the hermitage of ★★ **Nostra Senyora de Bonany**. Leave Petra in a southwesterly direction along the road signposted to Felanitx, passing the old mill tower of Joan Valero on the way. From here it is another 4km (2½ miles) to the top of the 317-m (1,040-ft) high **Puig de Bonany**.

The view from the cross

After Miquel Vicens, a priest from Petra, had recovered from a serious illness, he had a chapel built on this hill, and when the people of Petra prayed here for a good harvest during the famine year of 1609, their prayers were answered. The first hermits arrived in 1896, and the present church was built on the site in 1925, though the main portal of the original structure (1789) has been retained. The large building has two bell towers, a barrel vault and a high dome above the crossing. The colourful wooden statue of the Virgin on the altar is flanked by St Paul and St Anthony. Outside there is an attractive old well in the middle of the courtyard, and the view from the terrace extends far across the surrounding Pla de Mallorca with its almond and carob orchards. Up to 20 different towns can be seen from here on clear days. There are five simple cells here for overnight accommodation (bring a sleeping bag or blankets).

The route leads back to the north now, past fields full of almond trees, as far as the town of **Santa Margalida**, known as Hero to the Romans, and as Abenmaaxbar to the Moors. It was raised to the status of a villa as early as 1232. The town is on a small rise and can be seen from afar. The ★ **church of Santa Margalida** has a magnificent high altar, and in the Capilla San Antonio is a 13th-century statue of St Margaret. The magnificent Capilla Santo Cristo de las Animas with its valuable golden shrine is by the sculptor Tomás Vila (1947). Catalina Thomàs, Mallorca's patron saint, is particularly revered in Santa Margalida. There has been a procession here in her honour on the first Sunday in September for the last 100 years.

The PM341 leads from Santa Margalida straight to the bay of Alcúdia and Can Picafort, a large resort area particularly popular with Germans. The range of entertainment here is vast, but the place has little charm of its own. Not far away from Can Picafort, beyond the suburb of Son Bauló (take the C712 for about 2km/1 mile in the direction of Artà), is the Phoenician necropolis of **Son Real**. The slender cement obelisks with red tips near the yachting harbour are of far more recent origin – troops used them for target practice during the Franco regime. Off in the direction of Port d'Alcúdia are the attractive sand dunes of Muro, and solitary corners are quite easy to find here, even in peak season.

Grazing in S'Albufera

Pass the Platja de Muro now on the C712 in the direction of Port d'Alcúdia. Just before the first hotels start to appear, the road reaches a canal crossing the ★★ **S'Albufera d'Alcúdia** (daily 9am–7pm, winter 9am–5pm), a huge area of marshland (2,500ha/6,170 acres) between Port d'Alcúdia, Sa Pobla, Muro and Can Picafort. It is separated from the sea by an 8-km (5-mile) long and 500-m (1,600-ft) wide strip of sandy beach. The Mallorcans call this area Albufera Gran, to distinguish it from Albufera Petit near Pollença. Numerous canals criss-cross the area, and there are also two rivers, the Torrent d'Almadrà and the Torrent Sant Miquel. In 1863 John Frederick Bateman and William Hope, co-owners of the New Majorca Land Co., bought the entire area and began to reclaim large sections of it for agriculture. This was when most of the canals and irrigation facilities were built. In 1901 a firm from Valencia began cultivating rice and shortly afterwards a paper factory appeared. From 1946 to 1976 there were salt-works here.

Today this marshy area is a paradise for migratory birds, and many smaller creatures live here too, including turtles, snakes and eels, and several rare species have been claiming the attention of international specialists. In 1988, 1,700ha (4,200 acres) of S'Albufera were declared a nature reserve, and a new information centre was opened in 1994 to mark the reserve's fifth anniversary. Hiking trails, cycle paths, picnic sites, bird-watching stands and pony-and-cart trips are just a few of the pleasant surprises in store for the nature lovers who come here.

The marshes are a paradise

The Artistic Legacy

Megalithic monuments

The first inhabitants of Mallorca occupied the island between about 1300 and 1000BC. Having left behind no written texts or paintings, the most visible legacy of their presence were the large number of mysterious round towers (*talayots*) that once dotted the island. Constructed of large blocks of stone, these towers were the focal point of prehistoric settlements. While the *talayots* could have performed some burial or other ceremonial function, experts believe that their primary purpose was defensive. The quantity of arms found at a number of sites indicates that while the people of the so-called Talayotic culture may well have carried on primitive but active trade with others around the western Mediterranean, their primary concern at home was fending off the attentions of aggressive neighbours. Every settlement was in a constant state of readiness, and every settlement was surrounded by a massive Cyclopean wall for protection.

These remarkable remnants of the megalithic era are no longer a very common feature of the Mallorcan landscape. Over the centuries they became a ready source of valuable stone, used by farmers for constructing walls and builders for their churches and palaces. Nevertheless, two settlements are well worth a visit: Ses Països in the north (*see page 71*), and Capocorb Vell in the south (*see page 67*).

From the Romans to the Modernists

The best places to find archaeological remains dating from the Roman occupation are Pollença and Alcúdia; the finds are on display in Alcúdia's archaeological museum. In contrast, the museum in Manacor contains mosaic fragments from the Early Christian basilica of Son Peretó. The Almudaina Arch and the Arab Baths (Banys Arabs) in Palma's Old Town date from the Moorish occupation, as do the Alfàbia Gardens (and the magnificent panelling in the entrance hall of the manor house there), the ruined castle at Alaró and the ruined fortress of Castell del Rei.

Roman bridge at Pollença...

... and remains at Alcúdia

The Christian conquest of the island under James I of Aragon saw the construction of several important sacred and secular buildings, which included the cathedral and the Consulate of the Sea in Palma. During the 18th and 19th centuries, the island's wealthier landowners and nobles had large manor houses built on their land. These were surrounded by ornamental gardens, and their facades and interiors are often magnificent. Large palazzi, with idyllic patios (inner courtyards), were also built in the towns.

Palma cathedral

At the beginning of this century the Catalan version of art nouveau known as Modernisme made its appearance on Mallorca, and there are several fine Modernist facades in Palma. The finest example, though, is doubtless the Gran Hotel, which has now been converted into an artistic and cultural centre.

The Art of the Margers

The honey-coloured stone walls in the middle of the island are a fine sight in the sunshine. The men who so painstakingly built them are known as *bancaleros* (Castilian) or *margers* (Catalan). The stone used to build them is either quarried or collected from the surrounding fields, and the design of the wall is completely unplanned. The wall-builder has to assemble the whole thing rather like a jigsaw. Mortar isn't used for the traditional stone wall, instead the big stones are placed at the bottom to act as foundations, and the centre is filled with lots of smaller stones. Finally, the *marger* looks for the finest and roundest stones to round off his work.

If a wall collapses or is damaged, perhaps because a car runs into it, all the small stones pour across the road. Repairs are difficult and expensive. Professional wall-builders are hard to come by these days, and earn around £20 a yard – one reason why many old traditional walls are being replaced by modern wire-mesh fencing. Along the smaller country roads in the middle of the island, however, the old stone walls with their *barreres* (wooden gates) are still an integral part of the landscape.

Sculpture in the Hort del Rei Gardens

At the Miró Foundation

Painting and sculpture

The works of leading Mallorcan sculptors and painters of past centuries can be admired today in museums and churches across Mallorca. Contemporary artists have

mainly drawn inspiration from the island's natural beauty. It all began with the Pollença School, of which one of the most famous exponents was the Catalan artist Anglada Camarasa. He lived from 1913 to 1956 in Port de Pollença, and his works can be admired today in the Gran Hotel in Palma. The Catalan painter and sculptor Joan Miró fled to Mallorca to escape the Franco regime, settling here in 1945 with his Mallorcan wife Pilar. The landscape was a source of continual inspiration to him, and he worked indefatigably in his studio in Cala Major, soon becoming Mallorca's (and Spain's) most famous artist and sculptor. Miró's works can be admired at several locations in Palma, notably the new Miró Foundation on the outskirts (*see page 27*).

Miró on display

The best-known of the younger generation of painters is Miquel Barceló, who was born in Felanitx in 1956 and is today one of the celebrated Spanish avantgardists. The works of many famous and not-so-famous Mallorcan artists can be seen in the numerous galleries, foundations, and exhibition halls in Palma. The island's capital isn't the only place to make such discoveries, however. One worthwhile establishment to visit among several elsewhere on the island is the S'Estació arts centre in Sineu.

Music

Mallorca has a lively classical music scene, with the Ciutat de Palma Symphony Orchestra performing many well-known works throughout the winter season. The opera season begins at the end of March in the Teatre Principal, and Menorcan singer Joan Pons is often on the programme. There are also regular concert series held in the various cultural centres in Palma (Sa Nostra, Gran Hotel, Fundació March, etc). The summer is the time for music festivals, which include the classical music festival at Deià, the sunset concerts in Son Marroig, the famous Chopin Festival at Valldemossa (*see page 37*), the Pollença summer festival and the Bunyola classical music festival. Almost all classical music concerts on Mallorca are held in monasteries or churches.

Chopin's piano

As far as local contemporary music is concerned, the 'Els Valldemossa' brothers are one of the most well-known folk groups on the island. They have been playing traditional music and old Mallorcan songs for over 40 years. The Mallorcan hymn *La Balanguera* is as much a part of their repertoire as a series of songs in honour of the Austrian Archduke Ludwig Salvator (*see page 38*). Another well-known interpreter of Mallorcan songs is Maria del Mar Bonet.

Mallorca also has its own version of the bagpipes, known as *sa xeremía*. They can be heard at village festivals, usually accompanied by fife and drums.

Festivals and Folklore

Mallorcan folklore evenings with music, dancing and singing are a regular feature at the island's larger hotels and holiday resorts. The traditional folk festivals in the smaller villages are a more authentic way of experiencing the island's customs. During these celebrations, Mallorcan music groups parade through the streets, there is folk dancing (in traditional costume) in the village squares, and the Dimoni (Mallorca's version of the devil, an important figure in local folklore) is often encountered.

Folk dancing routine

Here is a brief list of some of the more important annual festivals:

January 5: Three Magi Procession in Palma; **17**: Sant Antoni Abat festival in Artà, Sa Pobla and Manacor; **14–23**: Sant Sebastià festival in Palma.

February Vuelta ciclista a Mallorca cycle race; international organ week at church of Santa Eulàlia, Palma; carnival in Montuïri.

March Clay goods fair at Marratxí; golf tournament at Son Vida Golf Club near Palma.

April Mostra de Cuina Mallorquina culinary week in Palma; agricultural show at Santa Maria del Camí; Fira del Ram, palm festival in Palma.

Good Friday Processions in Sineu and Pollença.

May 1: Agricultural show in Sineu; **9–11**: 'Brave Women of Sóller' festival in Sóller; *end of May*: spring festival in Manacor.

June Palma book fair; Corpus Christi festival in Pollença; **23**: Festivals of St John in various towns; **29**: Fiesta in Porto Petro, procession on the water.

July Cala Rajada summer festival of classical music; folk dance festival in Palma; international folklore festival in Sóller; Pollença Festival (classical music in the monastery of Santo Domingo; Deià Festival (classical music).

Valldemossa

August Chopin Festival at Valldemossa; Montuïri fiesta; San Agustí fiesta in Felanitx.

September *First Sunday*: Processó de la Beata in Santa Margalida; Bunyola music festival; *last Sunday*: Binissalem wine festival.

Local crafts

October 16/17: patron saints procession in Palma; Alcúdia cattle and crafts festival; historic organ week in the island's churches; agricultural fairs in Campos, Felanitx and Llucmajor.

around November 14: craft fairs in Inca and Pollença.

December 31: festivities in Palma commemorating the Christian reconquest of the island under King James I.

Balearic slingers

In the Hort d'Es Rei gardens beneath the Almudaina Palace in Palma is the statue of the Balearic Slinger. The use of the slingshot is a national pastime; popular in antiquity, it has recently been revived and can be admired every Wednesday afternoon at around 6pm in the Bar España, Carrer Oms, in Palma, when the *foners* or *honderos* assemble in order to indulge in this rediscovered antique art. Several slingshot clubs have been formed, their members meeting up in large open spaces to practise.

The people of the Balearic Islands were famous for their accuracy with the sling even before the advent of the Romans. Hannibal had slingers in his army, and their services were rewarded with wine and women.

Mallorcans used to learn the art in their early youth, and this appears to be the case again today, as most slingshot specialists are under 20. They regularly organise public displays and contests, and don't mind anyone coming along to watch. The experienced keep a respectable distance from the beginners, however, as shot number one often 'backfires'.

Food and Drink

Tapas are small hors d'oeuvres (meat or fish delicacies with high-calorie sauces, mushrooms and omelettes in all kinds of variations) eaten by the Mallorcans in bars at regular intervals during the day, and followed by an enormous family meal in the evening. One popular speciality is *Pa amb Oli*, pronounced *pamboli*, which is a thick slice of toasted country bread rubbed with garlic, salted, and then sprinkled with top-quality olive oil. It comes with sliced tomato, cheese or mountain ham. *Sobrassada*, a pork sausage which has a sharp delicious taste and can be spread on bread, also makes a good snack.

Those after genuine Mallorcan cuisine (*cuina Mallorquina*) should head inland from the coast. First the wine arrives, accompanied by unsalted country bread and some spicy olives. A proper Mallorcan meal might begin with *frit mallorquí* (a kind of meat and vegetable stew), or *tumbet* (vegetable soufflé). Another very popular dish is *llomb amb col* (pork with cabbage and raisins). *Sopas Mallorquinas* isn't soup, but a substantial stew containing cabbage, bread and small pieces of pork. Another delicious and inexpensive Mallorcan dish is *arròs brut* (chicken or pork with rice), sometimes served as *arròs a la marinera* (a fish soup with rice). The most expensive kind of soup is undoubtedly the *caldereta*, either *de marisc* (with crustaceans) or *de llangosta* (with shrimps).

Genuine Mallorcan fare

89

Fresh seafood is a luxury on Mallorca: the sea around the island has been fished empty. Beef and game are also a rarity, though in autumn wild rabbit, roast pig and fresh mushrooms are eaten. For pudding, try almond ice cream and *gató* (almond cake), or the spicy *queso mahonés* from neighbouring Menorca.

Sweets galore

Since wine production on Mallorca is limited, menus usually feature bottled wines from Rioja, Navarra or Catalonia. Mallorcan reds contain at least 12 percent alcohol, and are either served in bottles from Binissalem or in clay jugs as *vi de la casa*. The region around Felanitx produces some superb white wines. As an aperitif, though, Mallorcans will usually drink a glass of Palo, a liqueur made with caramelised sugar that the locals revere as a panacea for just about everything.

Island wines and liqueurs

There's no better place to sample Mallorcan specialities than in a *celler* – a former wine cellar converted into a restaurant. The little town of Campos has one of the oldest *cellers* on the island, and the ones in Inca and Sineu are also justly famed. The Celler Sa Premsa in Palma is very good, as is the Can Amer, in the middle of Inca, which has made a name for itself with its fine blend of rustic decor, Mallorcan ambiance and delicious local cuisine, washed down with island wines.

Restaurant selection

The restaurants listed below are suggestions for a few of Mallorca's popular spots. They are divided into three categories: $$$ = expensive; $$ = moderate; $ = cheap.

The Bar Bosch in Palma

Palma
$$$Caballito del Mar, Passeig Sagrera 5 (near La Lotja), tel: 971 721074. Specialises in fresh fish and seafood. **$$$Es Parlament**, Conquistador 11, tel: 971 726026. Try the rice and paella dishes; beautiful dining room. **$$Celler de Sa Prensa**, Pl. Bisbe Berenguer de Palou 8, tel: 971 723529. Rustic *bodega* serving Mallorqui specialities. **$Na Bauçana**, Santa Bàrbara 4, tel: 971 721886. Vegetarian restaurant for breakfast and lunch, situated between the Gran Hotel and the post office. **$La Bóveda**, Boteria 3, tel: 971 714863. *Tapas* bar behind La Lotja.

Valldemossa

Valldemossa
$$Ca'n Costa, on the road to Deià, tel: 971 612263. Mallorqui cuisine in the rustic setting of a converted oil mill. **$Sa Costa**, Carrer de Jovellanos, tel: 971 612169. Simple restaurant adjacent to the monastery with good *tapas*.

Sineu
$$Celler Can Font, Carrer des les Roses, tel: 971 520313. **$$Moli den Pau**, Ctra. Sta. Margarita 25, tel: 971 855116. In an old windmill, serving local specialities.

Port de Sóller
$$$La Llotja del Pescador, by the harbour, tel: 971 867077. Renowned for its fresh fish.

Sa Calobra
$$Es Vergeret, Cala Tuent, tel: 971 517105. Mallorcan specialities on a terrace overlooking the sea.

Algaida
$$Cal Dimoni, Palma–Manacor Rd, tel: 971 665035. Grilled meat and sausages, *frit mallorquí* and *Pa amb Oli*.

Inca
$$Celler Can Ripoli, J. Armengol 4, tel: 971 500024. A *celler* that is more than 300 years old.

Torre de Canyamel
$$Sa Porxada, Torre de Canyamel, tel: 971 841310. Specialities on the grill, including excellent suckling pig.

Deià
$$$La Residencia, Camí Son Canals, tel: 971 639370. Hotel with exquisite restaurant in 16th-century mansion.

Active Holidays

Water sports

Diving, water-skiing, windsurfing, sailing, paragliding... Whatever sport it happens to be, Mallorca provides it. Boats and surfboards are available in all the larger resorts. Sailing trips can sometimes lead to marvellous deserted bays. Water-sport courses are offered in Port d'Andratx, Port de Pollença and Port de Alcúdia. Larger sailing boats and yachts (with or without skipper and crew) can be hired from Cruesa Mallorca Yacht Charter in Palma (tel: 971 282821). The high point of the sailing season is the Copa del Rey in August.

The art of windsurfing

Water amusement parks

The island's many water amusement parks, featuring water chutes, paddling pools and playgrounds, are ideal for families with children. Try any of the following: Aquapark (between Cala Figuera and Magaluf), Hidropark (Port d'Alcúdia), Aqua City-Park (between Palma and S'Arenal), Aqualandia (between Palma and Inca), or Marineland (off the Palma–Peguera motorway).

Water baby

91

A relatively new and unusual attraction is a trip on the submarine Nemo. It starts at Magaluf, and offers visitors the chance to observe the undersea world through its 22 portholes at a depth of 40m (130ft).

Golf

Mallorca is ideal for golfers. Beautiful natural landscape, nine courses and good weather are just a few of the advantages. The oldest course, opened in 1964, is at the Club Son Vida near Palma. The courses are open all year round.

Hiking and climbing

Hiking and climbing holidays on Mallorca are increasingly popular. A week's hike with an experienced guide is no longer a rarity, but good boots and overall physical fitness are important prerequisites. Simple hikes in the flatter parts of the island can be undertaken alone, but guides are essential up in the Serra de Tramuntana, where walkers face differences in height of up to 800m (2,600ft). The main dangers are sudden rainstorms and deep ravines.

Cycling tours

Cyclists can find all levels of difficulty on Mallorca. The flat stretches of coast in the north, the nature reserve of Albufera at Alcúdia, and the island's flat interior present no trouble. The northwest coast, however, has marvellously steep parts for the ambitious. Every kind of bicycle, including mountain bikes (and even Harley-Davidson motorcycles), can be hired at the resorts.

Easy rider

Getting There

By air

Taking the plane to Mallorca is quick, comfortable and inexpensive. There's a huge choice of flights, both charter and scheduled. Prices vary according to season. Cheap return tickets are often offered by the major carriers.

The holiday's end

By sea

Those travelling to Mallorca by train, car or bus have to board the car ferry in Barcelona, which can be reached by motorway. It's also possible to go by Motorail for some of the way. Taking the price difference into account, a trip to Mallorca by car rather than the charter plane/hire car option is only financially worthwhile for those planning to stay longer than three weeks.

Getting Around

By car

The island has around 1,600km (990 miles) of road. The most important routes branch out from Palma in star formation – the busiest are those leading to the airport, Andratx, Santanyí, Pollença, Alcúdia, and Manacor. The risk of accidents on narrow country roads and along steep sections of coast is high. Those eager to enjoy the view should avoid taking any risks and park first before doing so.

93

Hairpin bend at Formentor

When driving on the island remember that motorcyclists signal a right turn by holding up their left arm. Always have your driving licence and passport with you. Highway police levy fines on the spot for non-use of seat belts and sometimes operate speed traps.

By hire car

All the major international car rental companies have an office at the airport. Mallorcan companies provide airport pick-up service too, and it's worth comparing prices. The average daily rate is between 3,000 and 5,000 ptas including comprehensive insurance.

Parking

Looking for a parking space in Palma can be very tiresome. In the centre the so-called *ora* system is used: parking vouchers with a maximum period of 90 minutes. Alternatives are the car parks on the Plaça Major, the Plaça Rosselló (Olivar market), the Parc de Mar and also the free spaces on the Plaça Espanya. Drivers of rental cars keen on sightseeing tend to leave their cars in silly places along narrow country roads, thus disrupting bus traffic. There's usually somewhere sensible to park not far away.

By bus

Most bus routes begin in Palma, but the smaller villages are also well-connected with one another. There are far fewer buses during the winter season (1 November until 30 April), and some lines cease operations entirely. Almost all buses begin their journeys on Palma's Plaça Espanya or the streets surrounding it.

By taxi

Palma has several taxi ranks, or cabs can be hailed on the street with a wave. The moment the driver switches on the meter the basic rate appears, and the final price depends on the number of kilometres driven. Taxis in and around Palma are cheap compared to other European locations. Extra charges are normal for items of luggage and trips to and from the airport. Trips across the island, however, are very expensive. The official prices are posted at all cab ranks, and drivers also carry a list. For a cab in Palma, tel: 971 401414. At resorts, cabs can be ordered at hotel reception.

Boat excursions are fun

By boat from island to island

There are boat excursions from most harbours to local sights. Regular ferry services run between Palma and Ibiza, Palma and Maó, Alcúdia and Ciutadella and between Cala Rajada and Ciutadella. For information and reservations contact Tourist Information (*see opposite*) or a travel agent.

By train

Mallorca has two railway lines, both starting at the Plaça Espanya in Palma. The state-run *Tren de Isca* (tel: 971 752245) connects Palma with Inca 20 times a day, stopping at Marratxí, Santa Maria del Camí, Consell and Binissalem. From Inca there are regular bus services to Lluc Monastery and the surrounding area. The privately-owned Sóller railway (tel: 971 752051) makes five trips a day along the scenically stunning rail route (with plenty of tunnels) between Palma and Sóller, stopping at Son Sardina and Bunyola. The journey takes around an hour. From Sóller there are local bus connections to Deià, Valldemossa and Andratx.

All aboard the Orange Express

The Palma-Sóller railway is highly recommended. The train's first-class carriages are equipped with leather seats, mahogany panelling and brass fittings. If there isn't a seat available in either first or second class, travellers can enjoy a splendid view of the passing landscape from the little platform between the carriages. From Sóller the journey can be continued on the famous old tram known as the Orange Express, which takes its passengers through groves of aromatic citrus fruit to the port of Sóller 5km (3 miles) away.

Facts for the Visitor

Winding down

Travel documents

For stays not exceeding three months, citizens of the European Union, the US, Canada and Australia need bring only their passports. A residence permit has to be applied for where longer stays are involved.

95

Customs regulations

Since the latest European-Union regulations came into force in 1993, there are (generally speaking) no limits. Items for personal use may be brought in to the country duty-free. For consumer goods the following limitations apply: 800 cigarettes, 200 cigars, 1kg of tobacco, 90 litres of wine and 10 litres of spirits per person.

No shortage of souvenirs

Tourist Information

In the UK: Tourist Office of Spain, 57 St James's Street, SW1A 1LD, tel: 0171-486 8077.

In the US: Tourist Office of Spain, 665 Fifth Avenue, New York NY 10022, tel: 212-759 8822, fax: 212-980 1053; 8383 Wilshire Blvd, Suite 960, Beverly Hills, Ca 90211, tel: 213-658 7188, fax: 213-658 1061.

In Palma:
Consell de Mallorca, at airport Arrivals building.
Gobern Balear Tourist Office, Jaime III 10.
Fomento del Turismo de Mallorca, Constitución 1.
Palma Municipal Tourist Offices are located at Santo Domingo 11, and Plaça Espanya.

Exchange regulations

There is no limit on the number of pesetas that can be brought into the country, nor on the amount of foreign

currency (though very large sums should be declared). Money not exceeding 500,000 ptas in value may be taken out. For larger sums, special application has to be made.

Money

The Spanish unit of currency is the peseta (pta, ptas). There are 10,000, 5,000, 2,000 and 1,000 ptas banknotes, and 500, 200, 100, 50, 25, 10, 5 and 1 pta coins. It's a good idea to exchange money for pesetas while in Mallorca rather than back home (up to 3 percent saving). Watch the size of the commission charged when money is exchanged (cash, cheques, credit cards, etc): it can often amount to 5 percent of the sum transacted. Automatic tellers which accept most major credit cards will provide money at any time of day or night.

Opening times

Banks: Monday to Friday, 9am–2pm.
Shops: Usually 9am–1pm and 4.30–7pm. The larger supermarkets on the outskirts of Palma are open 10am–10pm. Shopkeepers in the resorts stay open during lunchtime and also late into the evening.
Restaurants: Food is not usually served before 1pm for lunch and 8.30pm for dinner. Sometimes closed on Sunday evening and on Monday.
Museums: Opening hours vary tremendously. Usually closed on Saturday, Sunday and/or Monday. Art galleries and craft shops in smaller towns are open only in the late afternoon from around 5pm onwards.
Government offices and institutions: normally open on weekday mornings only.

Souvenirs and markets

Mallorca's famous artificial pearls are manufactured in the town of Manacor. Their production can be observed by visitors to the factory, and the results can then be admired and purchased at sales halls. Clay pottery is another traditional craft. There are two main types of traditional cooking vessel on Mallorca: *ollas* (round) and *greixoneras* (rather flatter). Both are ideally suited to the preparation of Mallorcan stews, but should be heated only over an open flame. They also make good salad bowls.

Glass-blowing is another ancient art that has been given a new lease of life with the advent of tourism. The Vidrerías Gordiola near Algaida has several fine examples in its historic glass museum. Other glass foundries are La Menestralia near Campanet and La Fiore near S'Eglaieta on the road between Palma and Valldemossa. Weaving is also well represented, and the island's famous white decorative cotton material with its colourful motifs is best bought either in Pollença or Santa Maria del Camí.

Siurells are small baked-clay figurines based on Phoenician and Carthaginian originals, depicting men on horseback, women, shepherds, giants, bulls. They are usually around 7–20cm (3–8 inches) high and the baked clay is striped or dotted with green, red or yellow paint. An extensive collection of these figurines can be admired at the Ethnological Museum in Muro.

Tipping

Even where prices are inclusive it is usual to tip waiters and taxi drivers an extra 10 percent or so. Porters, hairdressers, chambermaids and room service attendants should be given at least 200 ptas, and the same goes for tour guides and bus drivers on excursions and round trips. With taxis, round off the sum to the next 100-peseta amount. When paying for drinks in cash, leave at least some peseta coins (25–50 ptas) on the counter. Porters at the airport have fixed rates.

Post

The main post office on Mallorca is at Carrer Constitució 6 in Palma; all the smaller towns have their own. Always send important mail registered – the postal *expres* system is fast and reliable. Stamps (*sellos*) can also be bought at tobacconists and hotel reception desks.

Telephoning

In Palma, the central telephone office is located near the main post office at the corner of Carrer Constitució and the Passeig del Born. In all the main tourist centres there are telephone offices at which you pay after the call. International calls are cheaper between 10pm and 8am, as well as on Sundays; local calls on Mallorca and within Spain are cheaper after 5pm and cheaper still after 11pm. International calls may also be made from public telephones (*internacional*) using 25, 50 and 100 peseta coins, but phone cards (*tarjetas de telefónica*), available from all tobacconists and post offices, are much more practical. First dial 07, wait for the tone, then dial the rest of the code for the country you want (for the UK dial 07-44; US and Canada dial 07-1), followed by the city code and then the number itself. A beep announces the end of the call.

Calling home

Public holidays

Schoolchildren on Mallorca have summer holidays from 15 June to 15 September. The following official holidays are observed by all the regions:

New Year's Day; 6 January (Epiphany); Maundy Thursday; Good Friday; 1 May; 25 July (St James); 15 August (Assumption of the Virgin); 12 October (Discovery of

America); 1 November (All Saints' Day); 6 December (Constitution Day); 8 December (Immaculate Conception); 25 December (Christmas).

Clothing and equipment

Beachwear is fine for the hotel pool and garden, but be aware of local mores and avoid being 'underdressed' in places like Palma Cathedral. For boat trips, hikes and cycle tours, remember to take suntan lotion, and clothing to protect from the sun.

Hikers and climbers need to bring good sturdy shoes, woollen or cotton socks, and head and sun protection. A light rucksack, anorak and water bottle are also recommended. Hiking shoes should be 'worn in'. For bringing bicycles or other bulky sports equipment into Mallorca, check ahead with the travel agent or airline involved.

Disabled

More and more hotels are installing facilities for the disabled, though progress is still somewhat slow. The municipal transport authority EMT provides special bus services for wheelchairs and the severely handicapped. For information tel: 971 295700.

Bare essentials

Nudism

The monokini is not an exceptional sight either on beaches or at the poolside, but this type of display is still frowned upon by many of the more elderly locals. It's best, therefore, to put on a bikini top, even temporarily, when conversing with them. A certain degree of sensitivity towards hotel employees and waiters is also called for. Most nude bathers head for the Es Trenc naturist beach in the south of the island.

Television and radio

There are two public television channels in Spain: TVE 1 and TVE 2. Private stations have been allowed to compete since January 1990, which include Antena 3, Tele 5 and the Pay-TV channel Canal Plus. Sky TV is available on Mallorca via the Astra satellite.

Voltage

Most hotels have 220v AC, though some places still have 125v. Adaptors can be bought at all major airports.

Health

Tap water is in short supply on Mallorca and often poor quality. It's best to drink mineral water, which can be bought from supermarkets in plastic bottles. Sunscreens and lotions are also necessary, along with a pair of sandals to protect against hot sand, sharp stones and sea urchins.

Medical assistance

The local Red Cross will take care of minor beach injuries free of charge. All resorts have medical centres (*centros medicos*) with English-speaking staff. These privately-run institutions like to be paid in cash immediately (roughly £25 a consultation). Immediate medical assistance can be obtained by dialling 061. Chemists are open during normal shopping hours. For 24-hour services, check the local papers under *Farmacias* or the sign outside the chemist's door.

Crime

There's a relatively high risk of theft in Palma, so the following rules apply: never leave anything in your car, never carry more money on your person than you need, leave your passport or identity card at your hotel and watch out for pickpockets in crowds. Be especially careful when getting money out of automatic tellers. Be wary of *trileros* (people who play with dice or cups) in the city's busier squares – they can fleece curious passers-by in seconds. Don't allow yourself to be talked into down-payments for coach trips, or for time-sharing apartments.

Emergency numbers

Policía Nacional, tel: 091 (theft, muggings).
Policía Municipal, tel: 092 (traffic accidents, breakdown).
Bomberos (fire brigade) in Palma tel: 080, in Playa de Palma tel: 971 490460, in all other places tel: 085.

Diplomatic representation

Vice-Consulates in Palma de Mallorca:
Great Britain: Plaça Major 3a, tel: 971 712445 and 971 716048.
USA: Ave. Rei Jaime III 26, tel: 971 722660.

99

Spoilt for choice

Accommodation

There are around 1,000 hotels and 500 official apartments with a total of 250,000 beds on Mallorca. During July and August be sure to book any accommodation well in advance. Reservations can be made via the hotel directly or via central reservations (*see below*). Many hotels are closed between November and the end of March.

Royal holidays

A series of magnificent hotels with special character have joined forces under the name *Reis de Mallorca* (Kings of Mallorca). These establishments are distinctive for their architectural beauty, tasteful design and excellent service. The group so far contains 18 hotels of varying price range, from the simple Hotel Costa d'Or in the tiny village of Llucalcari to the La Residencia luxury hotel in the artists' village of Deià. All hotels in the association can be booked via central reservations (*see below*).

Finca holidays

Finca holidays is the new term for old-fashioned farm holidays. *Fincas* are the former estates on Mallorca, many of which have given up farming for good and have restored their buildings, adding swimming pools and sanitation, in order to rent out their rooms to tourists. Most *fincas* are set in beautiful surroundings, far from the sea, and are comfortably furnished, with an open fire, clay pots in the kitchen and old ploughs and pitchforks leaning against the old stone walls. *Finca* holidays can either be booked as a full package (including flight, transfer or rental car) from travel agents in the UK or via central reservations.

Central reservations for hotels, apartments, holiday flats, *fincas* and the Reis de Mallorca group of hotels: Central de Reservas de la Federación Empresarial Hotelera de Baleares, Aragón 215, E-07006 Palma de Mallorca, tel: 0034-971 706006, fax: 0034-971 470981.

Camping

There are two official campsites on Mallorca: Camping Platja Blava (Category I, all year round), Crta Artà, 23km (14 miles), tel: 971 537863; Camping Club San Pedro (Category I, May to October), Crta Artà–Port d'Alcúdia, 7km (4 miles), tel: 971 589023, in winter tel: 971 730365. Camping is also permitted in the grounds of Lluc Monastery. Apply at the monastery office.

Overnight stays at monasteries and hermitages

Many monasteries and hermitages provide simple accommodation, self-catering facilities or restaurant service. It's advisable to bring blankets or a sleeping bag.

San Salvador Monastery

Hotel selection

The following are hotel suggestions for some of Mallorca's popular spots. They are in three categories: $$$ = expensive; $$ = moderate; $ = cheap.

Alaró
$Can Tiú, Carrer Petit 11, tel: 971 510148. Hotel with 11 rooms and restaurant, open all year round.

Alcúdia
$Fonda Llabrés, Pl. de la Constitució, tel: 971 545000. Simple pension in the centre of the town.

Banyalbufar
$$$Mar i Vent, tel: 971 618000, fax: 971 618201. Commanding position above the sea. Tennis courts. **$$La Baronia**, tel and fax: 971 618146. Restaurant, sun terrace and pool, all rooms with balcony and sea view, friendly atmosphere.

Cala d'Or
$$Rocador, Marqués Comillas 3, tel: 971 657055; fax: 971 657751. Good quality hotel located above the beach of Cala Gran. **$Bienvenidos**, Bienvenidos 3, tel: 971 657074. On the way in to town. Reasonably priced, simple rooms.

Cala Figuera
$$Cala Figuera, San Pedro 28, tel: 971 645251. The best hotel in town. **$Oliver**, Berneregi 37, tel: 971 645127. Pleasant pension with restaurant on the way in to town. All rooms have a balcony.

Cala Millor
$$Gran Sol, Passeig Marítim 4, Cala Bona, tel: 971 585283; fax: 971 586571. Beach hotel with pool and sauna.

Cala Rajada
$$Casa Bauza, Mendez Nuñez 61, tel: 971 563844, fax: 971 818091. Well maintained and quiet. **$Cala Rajada**, Miguel Garau 4, tel: 971 563002. Some rooms have their own terrace and sea view.

Cala de Sant Vicenç
$$Molins, Cala Molins, tel: 971 530200; fax: 971 530216. Large beach hotel; a long favourite with British visitors.

Cap de Formentor
$$$Hotel Formentor, tel: 971 865300; fax: 971 865155. Fine hotel with many famous past visitors.

Alcúdia

101

Hotel Formentor

Can Picafort
$$$Baulo Pins, Sta. Margalida 28, tel: 971 850063; fax: 971 719976. Quiet hotel away from the beach.

Colònia de Sant Jordi
$$Playa, Major 25, tel: 971 655256. One of the oldest hotels on the island. Beautiful lobby full of memorabilia; terrace with view of the cliffs and sea. **$Hostal Colonia**, Gabriel Roca 9, tel: 971 655278. Rooms with balconies.

Deià
$$$La Residencia, Cami Son Canals, tel: 971 639011; fax: 971 639370. Beautifully furnished 16th-century mansion. Exquisite restaurant. **$$$Es Molí**, on the road to Valldemossa, tel: 971 639000; fax: 971 639333. Traditional luxury hotel, surrounded by lush vegetation. **$Miramar**, Can Oliver, tel: 971 639084. Quiet location on the hillside.

Estallencs
$Maristel, tel: 971 618529; fax: 971 618511. Open all year round, a member of the 'Reis de Mallorca' group.

Felanitx
$$$Vista Hermosa, on the road between Felanitx and Porto Colom, tel: 971 824960, fax: 971 824591. Luxury hotel with pool and tennis courts and gourmet restaurant.

La Granja
$$$Finca Son Ferrà. Majestic old mansion near Esporles. Comfortable accommodation for up to 13 guests.

Llucalcari

The Costa d'Or

$$Costa d'Or, tel: 971 639025. In a stunning location with a magic atmosphere; particularly popular among younger visitors.

Muro
$$Son Serra. *Finca* between Muro and Can Picafort. Old country house with modern bungalows and pool.

Orient
$$$L'Hermitage, tel and fax: 971 180303 (closed November to February). Situated 2km (1 mile) from Orient in the direction of Alaró, this fine hotel is housed in a converted 17th-century mansion. **$$La Muntanya**, Bordoy 6, tel: 971 615373. Restaurant serves local specialities.

Palma
$$$Son Vida, Urb. Son Vida, tel: 971 790000; fax: 971 790017. Exclusive golfing hotel outside the city in a 13th-

century castle. **$$$Majorica**, Garita 3, tel: 971 400261; fax: 971 405906. Traditional hotel on the waterfront. **$$Born**, Ave. Rei Jaume III, tel: 971 712942. In the Can Ferrandell palace, renovated 1993. **$$Cannes**, Cardenal Pou 8, tel: 971 726943. Quiet location near Plaça Espanya. **$ Ritzi**, Apuntadors 6, tel: 971 714610. Modest pension in Palma's food alley.

Poolside view in Palma

Port d'Andratx
$$$Villa Italia, Camino de San Carlos 13, tel: 971 674011; fax: 971 673350. Exclusive hotel overlooking the bay. Roman-style pool.

Port de Pollença
$$$Sins Pins, Av. Anglada Camarassa 77, tel: 971 867050; fax: 971 866264. Pretty hotel with private beach and terrace. Open all year round. **$$Miramar**, Av. Anglada Camarassa 39, tel: 971 866400; fax: 971 864075. Old-style hotel on the beach promenade.

Port de Pollença

Port de Sóller
$$Port de Sóller, Urb. Costa de la Atalaya, tel: 971 631700. On the hillside with views of the bay. **$$Los Geranios**, Platja El Repique, tel: 971 631440. On the beach. **$$ Baltix d' Avall**. Old *finca* situated on the 580-m (1,900-ft) high Mount Baltix. There are a total of seven rooms, three of them housed in the mill tower. Attractive swimming pool.

Randa
$$Es Recó de Randa, Sa Font 13, tel: 971 660997. Fine cuisine, friendly service, nice terrace.

Sineu
$$Sa Casa Rotja, tel and fax: 971 185027. Restored 19th-century *finca* situated to the north of Sineu.

Sóller
$$ El Guia, adjacent to the station, tel: 971 630227. In a 17th-century building. **$$Finca Can Ai**, Cami de Son Puça 48, tel: 971 632494. A beautifully restored building on an estate among the orange groves 3km (1½ miles) from Sóller.

Valldemossa
$$$Vistamar, 2km (1 mile) from Valldemossa on the road to Banyalbufar, tel: 971 612300; fax: 971 612583. Luxury hotel in a restored mansion with acres of gardens and nice pool. Open all the year round. **$$ Ca'n Mario**, Carrer Uetam 8, tel: 971 612122. Simple family hotel in the town centre.

Index